RUSTIC

RUSTIC

COUNTRY HOUSES
RURAL DWELLINGS
WOODED RETREATS

TEXT AND
PHOTOGRAPHS BY
BRET MORGAN

RIZZOLI
NEW YORK

First published in the United States of America in 2009 by
RIZZOLI INTERNATIONAL PUBLICATIONS, INC.
300 Park Avenue South, New York, NY 10010
www.rizzoliusa.com

ISBN-13: 978-0-8478-3300-9
LCCN: 2009924757

Cover: The Point (formerly Camp Wonundra), Saranac Lake, New York
Endpapers: Wawapek Farm, Cold Spring Harbor, New York
Frontispiece: Ames Gate Lodge, North Easton, Massachusetts
Opposite: Camp Topridge, Brighton, New York

Designed by Charlotte Staub
Printed and bound in China

2009 2010 2011 2012 2013 2014 / 10 9 8 7 6 5 4 3 2 1

CONTENTS

Mr. and Mrs. Lawrence J. Turnure, Jr. at Raquette Lake, New York, as photographed by Alonzo Mix in August of 1893.

INTRODUCTION

In August of 1893, Mr. and Mrs. Lawrence J. Turnure, Jr. were photographed as they relaxed in a lean-to shelter in the Adirondack Mountains. Some details of the lives of this glamorous young couple can be exhumed from the society columns of the Gilded Age. Lawrence was the son of a wealthy banker; he rode, played polo, and was one of the best-dressed young men in New York. His wife was a celebrated beauty, née Romaine Madeleine Stone. Her father was Brigadier General Roy Stone, a civil engineer specializing in road and railroad construction, and a military hero who distinguished himself in the Civil War and again in the Spanish-American War.

In short, Mr. and Mrs. Turnure were members of that upper crust of society that enjoyed the benefits of the rapid growth of industry and infrastructure in the decades after the Civil War, when the United States flexed its muscle as an economic power with imperial ambitions. One of these benefits was an abundance of leisure time that could be devoted to recreation—or to reflection, like Thoreau at Walden Pond—in spectacular natural settings far from the clamor of industry and the constraints of urban life. Another benefit was the ability to travel quickly and comfortably to these destinations on an ever-expanding network of railroads, the very symbol of the headlong rush of modern life that moved Thoreau to ask: "And if railroads are not built, how shall we get to heaven in season?"[1]

The architecture of leisure that developed in these picturesque corners of the natural world was influenced by the writings of landscape architect Andrew Jackson Downing, who proposed that "buildings of more irregular outline, in which appear bolder or ruder ornaments, and a certain free and rustic air in finishing, are those which should be selected to accompany scenery of a wilder or more picturesque character, abounding in striking variations of surface, wood, and water."[2]

The New York & Canadian Railroad carried passengers back to nature through a tunnel at Willsboro, New York, that was blasted through six hundred feet of Adirondack granite. Photograph by Seneca Ray Stoddard, c. 1876.
COURTESY OF DANIEL WAY.

Downing's theories took form in the shingled summer homes that rose from the New England coast, and in the camps that dotted the lakes of the Adirondacks. All were buildings that were sensitively adjusted to their terrain, and built of indigenous materials so that they seemed to grow out of their surroundings.

The ancient Vitruvian idea that architecture had begun when man first built a hut in the forest had been given fresh currency in the eighteenth century by Abbé Marc-Antoine Laugier; the frontispiece of his *Essai sur l'architecture* may be the best-known image of theoretical architecture ever published. The architect A. J. Davis turned the image of the primitive hut into a house with log columns in his "American Cottage No. 1," which he published in *Rural Residences* 3, the first American book about the design of country houses. Laugier's indirect influence can also be felt in Downing's sketches of rustic garden seats, arbors, and trellises.

Many of these designs were surely known to William West Durant, who began developing the artfully rustic architecture of the Adirondacks at Camp Pine Knot in 1878. A sophisticated architect manqué, Durant also drew inspiration from the American log cabin, the Swiss chalet, and the Japanese house. As professional architects—including Grosvenor Atterbury, William Coulter, William Scopes and Maurice Feustmann, and Kirtland Cutter—designed rustic buildings that exceeded the size and complexity of Durant's buildings at Camp Pine Knot, they recognized both the dimensional constraints inherent in true log construction and the spatial limitations of the dark and boxy interiors of the traditional chalet form. In response, they created a stylistic hybrid that combined the innovative spatial flow of Shingle Style planning with the straightforward construction and naturalistic materials of the Adirondack rustic.

The adaptability of this hybrid rustic style to a wide variety of settings is demonstrated by two houses on opposite sides of the country: Wawapek Farm on the North Shore of Long Island, and the Charles Millard Pratt House in Ojai, California. Both are superbly adapted to the topography, climate, light and mood of their settings. The fact that both were commissioned by clients who had spent considerable amounts of time vacationing in the Adirondacks is a telling indication of the new mobility of American society at the turn of the twentieth century.

The closing of the frontier, which was reported by the 1890 census, and the growth of tourism in the West coincided with the popularization of rustic architecture. No longer confined to the playgrounds of the well-to-do, it assumed a monumental scale in the design of exhibition buildings and hotels. A milestone in this development was the construction of the Idaho Building for the 1893 World's Columbian Exposition in Chicago.

Frontispiece of Abbé Marc-Antoine Laugier: Essai sur l'architecture, *Paris, 1755. Allegorical engraving of the Vitruvian primitive hut, after a drawing by Charles Eisen.*

Designed by Kirtland Cutter of Spokane as an immense chalet, the Idaho Building was constructed from trainloads of native logs and rock that were imported to Chicago. The entrance was a tunnel through the base of the building's immense central chimneystack.[4] In less than six months, the Idaho building received eighteen million visitors.

During this period, railroads sought to increase traffic on their transcontinental routes by building grandly rustic hotels amidst the awe-inspiring scenery of the West. The most striking of these is the Old Faithful Inn at Yellowstone; other noteworthy examples include El Tovar on the south rim of the Grand Canyon and the Many Glacier Hotel in Montana. After the National Park Service was established in 1916, its designers looked to these hotels for inspiration as they established guidelines for the naturalistic integration of large buildings into the landscapes of the parks.

As the chilly abstraction of International Style modernism became the leading architectural fashion of the 1920s and 1930s, rustic design was relegated to the bargain basement of architectural history. Except for a few unusual private commissions, such as Camp Wonundra on Saranac Lake, the survival of a traditional rustic aesthetic during the 1930s was dependent upon government construction of park facilities. A masterpiece of this rustic twilight was Timberline Lodge in Oregon, the last great public building to incorporate a wealth of handcrafted ornamental detail.

Two houses of the 1930s—Fallingwater in Pennsylvania and Fortune Rock in Maine—exemplify the development of an alternative modernism connected to the natural world, a modernism that incorporates many of the underlying principles of rustic design. Like earlier rustic buildings, these houses appear to grow from their surroundings, and their construction incorporates an abundance of natural materials.

Another alternative form of modernism developed in the Pacific Northwest, where several generations of designers created a spare new architecture of wood and glass inspired by the region's lush forests and rainy weather. Roland Terry was among Seattle's most accomplished designers in this idiom during the 1950s and 1960s; his weekend retreat in the San Juan Islands is a masterpiece of casual elegance.

The rise of Post-Modernism brought a return of traditional imagery to architecture. Robert Venturi's design of a ski retreat in Vail is a refined abstraction of the rustic past. More recently, other designers have embraced the sensuous materiality of log and stone construction, with results as varied and stirring as Robert A. M. Stern's neo-traditional design for Spruce Lodge in the Colorado Rockies, and Peter Bohlin's romantic rustic modernism at Ledge House in the Catoctin Mountains of Maryland.

Many Glacier Lodge, Glacier National Park, Montana, Thomas D. McMahon, 1914.
POSTCARD C. 1916. COLLECTION OF THE AUTHOR.

House in Vail, Colorado, Venturi & Rauch, 1977.
COURTESY OF VENTURI & SCOTT BROWN.

RUSTIC

AMES GATE LODGE

NORTH EASTON, MASSACHUSETTS

Henry Hobson Richardson
1880–1881

THE GATE LODGE that H. H. Richardson designed for the estate of Frederick Lothrop Ames ranks among the most influential works of rustic architecture in America. In the late nineteenth century, an era fascinated by geology and nature, the cyclopean rubble of the gate lodge caused a sensation. Richardson's expressive use of natural stone, and the poetic integration of lodge and landscape, were soon echoed in the shingled houses of New England, then in the great camps of the Adirondacks, and finally in the national parks of the West.

Appropriately enough, Frederick Ames' fortune had its origins in digging. His grandfather established a shovel factory in North Easton in 1803; by mid-century the Ames shovel was an essential tool used everywhere from the expansion of the Erie Canal to prospecting in the California gold rush. Ames' father and uncle—Oliver and Oakes Ames—became national figures as financiers of the transcontinental railroad. Frederick Ames followed his North Easton forebears into business, but he preferred to socialize among Boston's intelligentsia, where he was respected as a horticulturist, patron of the arts, and philanthropist. It was in these circles that he met Richardson and Frederick Law Olmsted, the visionary landscape architect.[1]

In 1877 Ames began an ambitious civic improvement program in North Easton. He commissioned a series of buildings by Richardson—a library, a town hall, and a railroad station—set in naturalistic landscapes by Olmsted. Ames turned again to Richardson and Olmsted in 1879, as he developed the grounds of Langwater, his summer home on the outskirts of North Easton. Richardson and Olmsted made plans for a new entrance drive, leading past Ames' celebrated greenhouses and gardens on the way to the existing manor house. A new lodge would mark the beginning of the drive, where it joined the public road.

The northern front of the gate lodge is a nearly continuous wall of stone. It runs parallel to the public road, neatly thwarting any attempt to peep into the estate, and compelling visitors to enter through the dramatic Syrian arch. Beyond the arch, a broad view of rolling lawns and towering trees is revealed to the visitor, but the manor house remains tantalizingly out of sight, hidden by a final bend in the drive.

The back of the lodge faces the sun and has a playful appearance. A porch and whimsical well tower protrude from the lodge; an upper porch and lower stairway are carved into it. The ground floor of the lodge housed the estate gardener; above were bedrooms for male guests at the estate and a spacious living hall. The living hall opens to the balcony of the well tower, allowing guests on the upper floor to draw water from below, or to wave to the distant manor house.

The lower wing across the drive contains a single dirt-floored room beneath a trussed ceiling, punctuated by an apsidal end. This gracefully proportioned space was used to overwinter Ames' specimen plants. Light pours through a horizontal range of windows in the south wall; a fireplace in the north wall provided heat. With the gardener living just across the drive, Ames' prized shrubs and fruit trees were pampered through the harsh Massachusetts winters.

The stone used to build the lodge was pulled from the grounds of the estate. Richardson relied on his longtime contractors, the Norcross Brothers, in the detailing of the walls, as Ames described in a letter of 1881: "The boulder walling frustrated architectural sketches and penciled plans and the formation of the walls demanded daily evaluation and decision as they were laid. The boulders were placed with attention to the textural effects radiated by the brute coarseness of the medium."[2]

The orange tile roof of the gate lodge is an early appearance of japonism in American architecture.[3] Boston's long tradition of maritime trade in East Asia made it a leader in America's growing interest in all things Japanese. Richardson's use of the swelling karahafu, or cusped gable, above the arch of the lodge may well have been a nod to the cultural sophistication of his client. Ames was an enthusiastic benefactor of Boston's Museum of Fine Arts, the preeminent American institution in the study of Japanese art.

When construction of the gate lodge was completed, Olmsted intensified the drama of Richardson's primeval architecture by treating the land around the lodge as a glacial moraine. Fieldstones were partially buried around the grounds, increasing in size and number as they approach the lodge, which commands this rough terrain like a glacier-scoured monument of the last ice age.

The eastern wing of the lodge contains a long, brightly lit room for the overwintering of plants.

GENERAL CHARLES G. LORING HOUSE

PRIDES CROSSING, MASSACHUSETTS

William Ralph Emerson
1881–1883

When the Ames family made their annual summer retreat to their North Easton fiefdom, many other upper class Bostonians took leave of the city to enjoy the cool breezes and salty air of the North Shore. Artists were among the first to explore and celebrate this rugged coast, among them Frederic Church, Fitz Hugh Lane, and John Frederick Kensett, who frequented the very cove where the Loring House was later built.

As artists drew attention to the North Shore, the Eastern Railroad followed in their path. In 1844, a handful of shrewd Bostonians began buying up the farms and pastures east of Beverly that would soon lie between the railroad tracks and the ocean. Among them was Charles Greely Loring, a prominent lawyer.

Loring bestowed parcels of land on family and friends, including his Harvard classmates, thereby marking his territory as a retreat for the "right sort" of people. While Manchester and Gloucester attracted tourists to hotels and boarding houses, such public establishments were never contemplated in Loring's domain. Prides Crossing—named after an old local family—developed as a realm of hushed exclusivity.

Loring's son, Charles G. Loring, Jr., was born in 1828. After graduating from Harvard, he traveled throughout Europe and the Middle East, contracting an abiding interest in Egyptian art and archaeology, as well as a respiratory ailment that forced his return to the North Shore to convalesce:

> He devoted himself to the laying out and carrying on of the seaside farm at Beverly, Massachusetts, since 1844 the summer home of the family. The love of flowers and of outdoor occupation which was thus awakened never forsook him, and in after life he often said that had he been born twenty-five years later he would have made the then also most unknown calling of a landscape gardener his profession.[1]

Opposite: The Loring House is approached very casually, from the back and on a decline. A lantern, nearly hidden in the ivy, marks the entrance to the arcaded porch.

Colonial Revival details, such as the fanlight over the front door,
were subtle reminders of the status of an old Boston family.

Like many sons of Boston's elite, Charles G. Loring, Jr. volunteered to serve in the Civil War. He rose from Lieutenant to Major General, evidence that this "reticent and retiring"[2] personality had become a determined leader. In the 1870s he devoted himself to Boston's new Museum of Fine Arts, and was named curator in 1876. In 1875 General Loring married Mary J. Hopkins; their daughter Ruth was born in 1877. Their son—Charles G. Loring—was born in 1880, but died at four months. A second son—yet another Charles G. Loring—was born in 1881. Perhaps in celebration of the birth of his healthy namesake, General Loring commissioned Boston architect William Ralph Emerson to design a summer cottage on the family estate at Prides Crossing.

The Loring House was planned with daring informality.
The arcaded approach to the front door leads past the
service quarters of the house, which are concealed behind
the high windows to the right.

The multi-level living hall is lit by an enormous
Palladian window overlooking the sea.

With its low ceiling, dark paneling and rough hearth, the dining room is a reminder of ancient colonial farmhouses.

Opposite: These curiously rough beams may have been inspired by the maritime past of the North Shore.

William Ralph Emerson, a distant cousin of Ralph Waldo Emerson, was a masterful innovator and practitioner of the Shingle Style. In the 1880s his practice boomed as he designed suburban estates around Boston, cottages along the North Shore, and vast summer mansions in Maine. The Loring House was one his finest achievements, and today it survives much as he designed it. Here the many innovations of the shingle style—a unity of house and setting, free and inventive planning, the direct use of natural materials—are all joined in a carefree celebration of the promise of informal summer living.

Emerson possessed a virtuoso talent for designing houses to realize the full potential of their settings. The Loring House was built atop a precipitous crag that towers over the sweep of Plum Cove. The site was left in its natural state, suggesting that both Emerson and General Loring (a landscape gardener manqué) were well aware of Frederick Law Olmsted's famous injunction against improving on nature: "For Heaven's sake, leave it alone!" [3]

The first floor was built of stone, so that the house appears to have been thrust out of the ground by a mighty geologic event. The upper floors and roofs are covered in shingles, a vernacular material that evokes memories of the old farms of the North Shore, and of the colonial roots of the Boston Brahmins.

The drive to the house climbs over a wooded hill, twisting at the top to pass between immense boulders. A visitor arrives very casually, at the back of the house. A broad porch angles past the service wing to the front door, offering just a glimpse of the view beyond.

The full impact of the setting is revealed only upon entering the house. The soaring living hall is flanked by the parlor on one side, and the dining room on the opposite. These principal rooms are laid out with the simplicity of a true cottage: they all face the ocean, and they all open broadly into one another. From wherever one stands within them, they offer both direct views and peripheral glimpses of the sea.

The living hall and the parlor were outfitted with windows that were unusually large for the period. The parlor, which offers the broadest views, is raised one step above the living hall, as if it were a viewing platform. The parlor contains a very early picture window: from any vantage point, it frames a composition of nothing but ocean and sky.

The dining room, designed for life after dark, has the low, sheltering quality of a colonial farmhouse. Within a paneled inglenook stands a hearth, its large stones set in a deliberately rustic manner. The inglenook is framed by bracketed beams that possess a curiously rough and nautical quality: a reminder, perhaps, of the maritime past of the North Shore.

After General Loring's death in 1902, his summer home and its contents were sold to Quincy A. Shaw, Jr., a Boston mining executive. Shaw added a sunroom and library, but did little else to change the original house. Samuel Codman inherited the house from his mother, Lydia Eliot Codman Shaw, in 1966. Codman, now a centenarian, has maintained the house with its original finishes, furniture and décor intact. He has helped organize a non-profit group, The Friends of the General Charles G. Loring House, to raise funds for Historic New England to acquire this remarkable property for serious study and public enjoyment.

Overleaf: The Loring House rises from stone foundations, like a natural extension of the steep bluff.

In the parlor, an early picture window frames the sea and sky.

CAMP PINE KNOT

RAQUETTE LAKE, NEW YORK

William West Durant

1878–1895

Twigs were applied over birchbark to create whimsical decorations.

Preceding overleaf: The largest and most impressive building at Camp Pine Knot is the Swiss Cottage. It began as a one-story log cabin in 1878; a second story, built of lumber clad with bark, was added in 1882. Inside were bedrooms for guests and a shared living room. The generously sized windows show the influence of Japanese shoji screens in the patterning of their delicate mullions. The Swiss Cottage was publicized in travel guides, and it became the prototype for buildings in many Adirondack camps.

Opposite: Like the structure of a primitive woodland lean-to shelter, the ceiling of Durant's cabin was made of peeled logs beneath a covering of birch bark.

This was the first of the artistic and luxurious camps that are so numerous today that the story of their multiplication might fittingly bear the title "Camps is Camps." But when Pine Knot rose among the stately trees on the lone shore of Raquette Lake, it was a new and unique blend of beauty and comfort. It became the show place of the woods.... Before it was built there was nothing like it; since then, despite infinite variations, there has been nothing essentially different from it.

A. L. Donaldson, *A History of the Adirondacks*, 1921

AS SHINGLED SUMMER HOMES rose from the rocky New England coast, another style of leisure architecture took shape around the lakes of far upstate New York: the Adirondack camp. Intrepid sportsmen had been hunting and fishing in the Adirondacks since the 1830s, but their accommodations were limited to tents and primitive lean-tos; the latter assembled by their backwoods guides from tree limbs, with peeled bark as a covering for the roof. The concept of a permanent recreational camp was still new when William West Durant, the impresario of the Adirondacks, gave it a distinctive architectural identity at Camp Pine Knot.

Durant had developed an affinity for design during an unusually cosmopolitan childhood. With his sister and their English-born mother, he was raised in Europe while his father, Dr. Thomas C. Durant, amassed a fortune building the Union Pacific tracks of the transcontinental railroad. After his education at Twickenham School in England and Bonn University, young Durant roamed Europe and North Africa as a discerning dilettante, until Dr. Durant lost much of his wealth in the Panic of 1873. Summoning his family home, he turned to his son for assistance in restoring the family's fortunes.

Dr. Durant's assets included more than 500,000 acres of Adirondack wilderness, at a time when the publication of William "Adirondack" Murray's *Adventures in the Wilderness; or, Camp Life in the Adirondacks* had excited the interest of vacationers in search of recreation in nature. When William Durant visited Raquette Lake in 1876 he recognized its potential for development as a resort. That winter he began the construction of a camp that he intended to serve as an inspiration for land sales to the very wealthy. The result was Camp Pine Knot, which was soon celebrated as "unquestionably the most picturesque and *recherché* affair of its kind in the wilderness."[1]

After his father's death in 1885, Durant pursued his vision of artistic camping with a perfectionism that required the demolition of a wall containing one misplaced stone, and with a business plan that amounted to little more than "if I build it, the millionaires will come." *The New York Times* chronicled his achievements at Pine Knot in 1894:

> "The original camp has been enlarged and with its several annexes and separate additions extends along the lake for over a quarter of a mile. There is nothing primitive about it, with its stained glass windows, unique rustic architecture and fine furnishings. It is provided with a piano, a library of 1,000 volumes, and every luxury that one could desire. Two French cooks and a retinue of 30 servants are kept here the year round for the entertainment of the guests who are so fortunate to share the hospitality of its owner."[2]

Durant's rustic enthusiasms were rooted in his sojourn in Europe. He had seen numerous authentic chalets; he may also have visited such rustic contrivances as Marie Antoinette's Petit Hameau and the follies erected on English estates by William Kent and others. Closer to home, inspiration was probably found in the essays of A. J. Downing, who praised the chalet as "the most picturesque of all dwellings built of wood … peculiarly adapted to a snowy country, rude in construction, and rustic and quaint in ornaments and details."[3] Downing's drawing of a tidy chalet adapted to American life bears a marked resemblance to the Swiss Cottage that became the iconic image of Camp Pine Knot.

In his treatise on picturesque landscaping, Downing included drawings of pavilions built from logs, branches, and even moss, "which from the nature of the materials employed and the simple manner of their construction, appear but one remove from natural forms."[4] It would have required only a small leap of imagination for Durant to associate such follies with the forest shelters assembled by the woodsmen of the Adirondacks, and to apply such craftsmanship to the sturdy outlines of the chalet.

Durant attempted to duplicate the success of Pine Knot by building two even grander camps, Uncas and then Sagamore; but his wilderness kingdom collapsed under a mountain of debt at the turn of the twentieth century. Ironically, when the bankrupt developer left the Adirondacks in 1904, his backwoods paradise for the superrich had become a reality. He had sold Pine Knot to Collis Huntington, Uncas to J. P. Morgan, and Sagamore to Alfred Vanderbilt. Development of the Adirondacks as a fashionable resort continued apace without Durant, but his influence lingered in the rustic architecture that was echoed again and again as new camps, now designed by professional architects, were built for Carnegies, Rockefellers, and Whitneys.

Durant's cabin at Pine Knot was lit by lanterns and equipped with a rustic outhouse with a view of Lake Raquette.

THE KILDARE CLUB

KILDARE, NEW YORK

William Scopes & Maurice Feustmann
1906

A dirt road leads through miles of old-growth forest to the remote Kildare Club.

Preceding overleaf: A broad porch shades the sunny southwest corner of the lodge.

WILLIAM SEWARD WEBB and his brother-in-law Frederick W. Vanderbilt founded the Kildare Club as a hunting preserve in 1882. Webb was the organizer of the Adirondack & St. Lawrence Railway, which opened much of the Adirondacks to development. At first the preserve could only be reached from the Raquette River over a rough wagon road, but after Webb connected the region to rail service from New York City in 1889, a private station was built just outside the preserve. From there, visitors were driven by horse and buggy, and later automobile, through miles of forest to the club's buildings on Jordan Lake.

By 1892 Webb's railroad was complete, and he was turning his attention to developing Nehasane Park, his vast property in the western Adirondacks. The Kildare Club was sold in 1896 to two sisters, Evelyn Lehman Ehrich and Harriet Lehman. Their father was Emanuel Lehman, a founder of Lehman Brothers, a commodities brokerage firm that evolved into a leading investment bank in the twentieth century. Evelyn's husband was Jules Ehrich, the owner of Ehrich Brothers, a department store on New York's fashionable "Ladies' Mile." Harriet was married to her first cousin Sigmund, a son of Mayer Lehman, another founder of Lehman Brothers. The Kildare Club kept its name but became a private family camp; today it belongs to third and fourth generation descendants of the Lehman sisters.

The Lehmans were one of many German-Jewish families drawn to the Adirondacks in the 1890s. Like other resorts of the era, the Adirondacks were exclusive, in the worst meaning of the word. The rules of the waspy Lake Placid Club were typical: they excluded anyone "against whom there is any reasonable physical, moral, social, or race objection ... This invariable rule is rigidly enforced: it is found impracticable to make exceptions to Jews or others excluded, even when of unusual personal qualifications."[1]

Beneath the lodge, a lean-to shelter hugs the shore of Jordan Lake.

Despite their prominence in business and their determined efforts at acculturation, affluent Jews were not accepted as social equals by most of their Gentile counterparts. Otto Kahn, the famously wealthy financier and courtly patron of the arts, summarized the situation with his definition of a too familiar epithet: "A kike is a Jewish gentlemen who has just left the room."[2]

A resort rife with prejudice was hardly suited to recreation and contemplation, so Jewish families built their own camps and clubs, often on lakefront sites purchased from W. W. Durant. The overextended impresario of the Adirondacks was pleased to do business with anyone possessing ready cash.[3] Many of this new generation of camps were designed by the prolific William Coulter. Around Saranac Lake, Coulter designed camps for Otto Kahn and industrial magnate Adolph Lewisohn, and the Knollwood Club for a membership that included mining tycoon Daniel Guggenheim, Louis Marshall, the lawyer and civil rights advocate, and George Blumenthal, the banker and philanthropist. Coulter favored the Alpine imagery that Durant had introduced to the Adirondacks, but he consolidated the functions of the many single-purpose structures of Camp Pine Knot and other early camps into multi-purpose lodges resembling substantial country houses.[4]

Nature is brought indoors by the taxidermist's art.

At Kildare, the original lodge of the Webb era burned in 1905, when a brother of Jules Ehrich fell asleep with a lit cigarette in his mouth.[5] It was quickly replaced by a structure designed in the new, consolidated manner by Scopes & Feustmann, an architectural firm in the nearby town of Saranac Lake.

The architects created a compact and practical building, well suited to a harsh climate and remote location. The principal rooms—dining room, living room, and a recreation room flanked by two master bedrooms—are arranged from south to north along the lakefront. Two perpendicular wings extend inland: the dining room connects to a south wing of kitchens and staff quarters; the north wing is devoted to family and guest bedrooms.

The two wings resemble twin chalets, with very little ornament. On the lakefront, the lodge shows a more eccentric face. The dining room is wrapped in a porch and crowned with a pyramidal roof, the living room bulges with a semi-circular window bay, and the recreation room steps forward with a broad chimney set between sizeable windows. In short, the exterior of the lodge is shaped by the volumes of the grand rooms within.

W. W. Durant's imaginative use of bark as a wallpaper is taken to a dizzy extreme in the cheerful living room.

Large windows brighten the dining room with light reflected from the porches just outside.

Opposite: The dining room celebrates the pleasures of eating, and hints at the horror of being eaten.

The Kildare Club has some of the finest rustic interiors in the Adirondacks. They remain remarkably intact after a century of use, thanks to owners who have valued history and tradition more highly than the fleeting pleasures of redecoration.

The barrel-vaulted recreation room was designed for days when inclement weather discourages outdoor activities. A wide fireplace is surrounded by banks of windows, a setting that allows family members to enjoy a campfire in a woodland clearing, without the bother of damp clothing, soggy kindling and wet matches. Much of the stylishly comfortable Arts and Crafts furniture in this room and throughout the lodge was manufactured by Gustav Stickley.

The living room is treated as an indoor rustic folly, with bark covering every inch of its walls and ceiling. The walls are hung with dozens of plaques of mounted fish, each with an inscription memorializing the fisherman and the date and location of his catch. Beams made of unpeeled logs support the ceiling and provide a habitat for two well-preserved black bears and a lonely beaver. Because the living room has windows in its opposite walls, it is the brightest and breeziest room in the lodge.

In the adjacent dining room, the interior walls are covered with shingles, as if the room were an exterior space turned outside in. In late afternoon the lowering sun fills the air with beams of deepening golden light; later the ceiling hovers like a night sky above the gleaming antler chandelier. The walk-in fireplace is decorated with an inscription taken from a ballad in Sir Walter Scott's "The Lady of the Lake."

> *Merry it is in the good greenwood,*
> *When the mavis and merle are singing,*
> *When the deer sweeps by, and the hounds are in cry,*
> *And the hunter's horn is ringing.*

Perhaps the most remarkable feature of the Kildare Club is its preserve of nearly 10,000 acres. One tract of 4,500 acres is the largest privately owned old-growth forest in the Northeast. It has never been logged, with the exception of white pines cut for ship masts during the Civil War. Successive generations of Kildare owners have been ardent conservationists, with the happy result that the property has become a boreal wildlife preserve. In springtime fawns graze within sight of the lodge, as the forest echoes with the jackhammering of woodpeckers. The current owners note that pileated woodpeckers, hairy woodpeckers, and the ineffable black-backed three-toed woodpecker are among the many species of birds that breed in the forest,[6] and they report with pride that the moose, which was exterminated from the Adirondacks in the nineteenth century, has returned to Kildare.

The recreation room includes a quiet alcove for letter writing. The lodge was furnished with Arts and Crafts furniture manufactured by Gustav Stickley.

Left: The recreation room was designed to banish gloom and boredom during the Adirondacks' frequent bouts of bad weather. Large windows admit abundant light, and the varnished ceiling bounces it around the room. The trophy mounts circling the walls testify to a belief held by conservationists in the early twentieth century that hunting served to refresh the city dweller by reminding him of his past as a noble savage in the wilderness.

Overleaf: Kildare's many bedrooms are furnished with a variety of old-fashioned twin beds. The large bedroom shown is one of two master bedrooms, both overlooking Jordan Lake, that reflect the club's dual ownership when the lodge was rebuilt in 1906.

Second overleaf: The porch off the dining room is lined with weathered rustic furniture. Before suntans became fashionable in the 1920s, an early fall retreat to the Adirondacks afforded women who had summered at the seashore an opportunity to restore their pale complexions before returning to urban society for the winter. Broad porches and comfortable furniture provided a shady setting for this ritual of enforced leisure.

CAMP TOPRIDGE

BRIGHTON, NEW YORK

Theodore Blake & Benjamin Muncil

1924

Among Adirondack terms calling for exact definition is the word "camp." And it calls loudly and somewhat despondently, as one who is lost; for if ever an exact little word gradually went to seed and ran wild, not only in a wilderness of mountains but in a wilderness of meanings, it is this one. If you have spent the night in a guide's tent, or a lean-to built of slabs and bark, you have lodged in a "camp." If you chance to know a millionaire, you may be housed in a cobblestone castle, tread on Persian rugs, bathe in a marble tub, and retire by electric light — and still your host may call his mountain home a "camp."

A. L. DONALDSON, *A History of the Adirondacks*, 1921

As THE ADIRONDACKS became a favored playground of the wealthy, showplace camps of such fanciful extravagance were built that the word "camp" nearly lost its meaning. Edward Litchfield, an avid hunter, built a stone pseudo-schloss and stocked its grounds with wild boar. After a voyage to the Far East, the Frederick Vanderbilts decided that Whiteface Mountain reminded them of Mount Fuji, rebuilt their camp as a Japanese village, and dressed their maids in kimonos.[1]

In the same year that Donaldson's tongue-in-cheek account of the plight of the word "camp" was published, Marjorie Merriweather Post bought Camp Kenosa from the heirs of Alvin Lothrop, co-founder of the Woodward & Lothrop department store of Washington, D.C. Dowdy old Kenosa was soon demolished and Camp Topridge, the most lavish and the most imaginatively rustic of all the showplace camps, was built atop its massive stone foundations.

Marjorie Merriweather Post was the only child of C. W. Post, founder of the Postum Cereal Company of Battle Creek, Michigan. When her father committed suicide in 1914, twenty-seven-year-old Marjorie inherited his fortune and began her transformation into the businesswoman, socialite, philanthropist and boxing enthusiast, who—after marital outings as Mrs. Edward Close, Mrs. E. F. Hutton, Mrs. Joseph Davies, and Mrs. Herbert May—preferred to be known as simply "Mrs. Post."

Opposite: The boat house offered visitors their first glimpse of Camp Topridge. The rest of the camp was hidden atop the thickly wooded ridge.

Overleaf: The boat house integrates structure and ornament in a tour-de-force of rustic naturalism.

Above: Outside the lodge, a screen door is decorated with Native American motifs in the bright colors favored by Marjorie Merriweather Post.

Right: The quiet exterior of the lodge serves to downplay its substantial size, and to magnify the surprise that lies within.

Overleaf: The living room was once densely cluttered with a world-class collection of Native American art and artifacts. After Mrs. Post's death, three moving vans moved the best elements of her collection to the Smithsonian Institution.

Post rotated with the seasons among a series of homes designed for lavish entertaining: a triplex penthouse high above Fifth Avenue, an English manor on Long Island, and, in Palm Beach, her fabled Hispano-Moorish estate, Mar-A-Lago. In Washington, D.C. she renovated a grand estate during her third marriage, and an even grander one after her third divorce. Although Post visited Topridge for little more than six weeks a year —to beat the late summer heat of New York, and later, of Washington—her camp was designed to match the splashy splendor of her other properties.

Like an Adirondack lido, Topridge was accessible only by boat. Visitors were greeted at the enchanting boat house, from which a funicular car ascended eighty feet to the lodge, atop a narrow hogback ridge. To the south of the lodge, luxurious cabins stretched along the crest of the ridge. North of the lodge was a neat village of service buildings, including accommodations for over eighty employees, a firehouse and a post office. Although Topridge is far larger than W. W. Durant's Camp Pine Knot, the deft dispersal of its many buildings along the narrow ridge lends it a similar meandering, episodic charm.

A Native American headdress hangs from a massive wrought iron firescreen.

Opposite: Boldly overscaled logs were used in the construction of a staircase and mezzanine within the living room.

Two unusual collaborators shared responsibility for the design of Topridge: Theodore Blake, an eminent New York architect, and Benjamin Muncil, an unlettered Adirondack builder. Blake was a designer in the distinguished office of Carrère & Hastings, where he collaborated in the design of both grand public buildings—notably, the New York Public Library, and the House and Senate Office Buildings—and of private estates for the likes of E. J. Harriman and Alfred I. duPont.

Ben Muncil was born into an impoverished Adirondack family. As a teenager he worked as a guide and caretaker, and began developing a talent for rustic carpentry. Although illiterate, he became a contractor by taking correspondence courses in architectural drawing, which his daughter read aloud to him.[2]

Blake supervised the planning of Topridge; Muncil oversaw construction and the detailing that gives the camp its deliciously rustic flavor. Muncil had a free hand in designing the grand entrance of the camp, the boat house. Its framing was assembled from carefully chosen cedar trees, which make an extraordinary decorative folly out of an essentially functional building. Muncil's gnarly masterpiece was the culmination of a tradition of rustic naturalism extending back to Camp Pine Knot.

Muncil was also involved in designing the living room that fills much of the lodge. Measuring 80 by 100 feet, it is the largest such room in the Adirondacks. To support its floating ceiling, Muncil employed a system of hidden trusses that he had devised for the great rooms of two earlier, nearby camps.[3]

Many of the characteristic motifs of Adirondack interiors were exaggerated to suit the scale of the living room. From the days of Durant, camps had been built with increasingly large windows, usually divided by muntins into smaller, inexpensive panes. At Topridge, some of the largest picture windows ever manufactured were installed in the opposite walls of the living room, framing panoramic views to the east and west. This modern fenestration contrasted with the markedly primitive atmosphere of the living room. Cavernous stone fireplaces anchored both ends of the room; a staircase and mezzanine were made of muscular logs.

Post was an unabashed collector of Native American artifacts. The finest rugs and blankets in her collection were exhibited in the living room, along with totem poles, an Eskimo kayak, and Geronimo's war bonnet. Towering over it all was an immense cigar-store Indian that Post had captured in New York City.[4] Furniture was covered in animal hides, and the floor was carpeted with wolf and bearskin rugs. A menagerie of stuffed local fauna—owls, foxes, beavers, and baby bears—looked on silently as two maids spent four hours a day dusting the hirsute room.

The comfortable sitting room of Mrs. Post's cabin.

The living room was the center of social life at Topridge. When a bell was rung from the lodge, guests assembled for cocktails in the living room dressed in tuxedos and gowns, as the hostess required. When the bell rang again, they proceeded into the adjacent dining room, where white-jacketed waiters stood at attention. Dinner was often followed by ballroom dancing, a favorite diversion of Post, who was celebrated for having once danced a lively tango with the aged John D. Rockefeller. On other evenings, first-run movies were shown. As the lights dimmed, Post distributed bat-hats to her female guests to discourage party crashing *chiroptera* from deranging their hairdos.[5]

Guests were housed in eighteen cabins; each with a sitting room, bedrooms, a thoroughly modern bathroom, and a screened porch. Each cabin was staffed with a footman and a maid, who could be summoned at the touch of a button. Local Adirondack woodsmen were available to lead visitors on hikes and portages, or to set up a cook-out in the lakefront lean-to; the eighty-five person staff of Topridge also included such non-rustic specialists as a barber, hairdresser, masseur, and dance instructor. Post famously welcomed her guests: "If there's anything you want and you don't ask for it, it's your own fault."[6]

Opposite: The low-lying cabins that housed Mrs. Post and her guests were tucked under pine trees at the edge of the ridge. Their screened porches and rear windows offered dramatic views of the water below.

The dacha is one of the few authentic log structures at Topridge.

When Post's third husband, the Washington lawyer Joseph E. Davies, served as Ambassador to the U.S.S.R. (1936–38), Post accompanied him to Moscow with her maid and masseur, thirty trunks, and fifty pieces of hand luggage.[7] Soon she was shipping home a vast collection of tsarist art seized from the aristocracy, which the cash-starved commissars were happy to sell at bargain-basement prices to finance Stalin's industrialization plan.

Upon their return to the U.S., Post had a replica of a Russian dacha built to serve as Davies' office at Topridge. The dacha sits comfortably among the camp's original cabins, a reminder of the many eclectic influences that have flavored Adirondack architecture from the very beginning, when Durant introduced subtle Japanese touches into the design of the windows of his iconic Swiss cottage at Camp Pine Knot.

After Post and Davies divorced in 1955, she emptied the Dacha and used it as a setting for her new terpsichorean enthusiasm: square dancing. The hostess and her guests do-si-doed around the barn-like room to the strains of a fiddle and banjo and the commands of a country caller.

The current owner of Topridge has restored the dacha to its original use as an office.

Onion domes, the traditional ornamentation of Russian Orthodox churches, decorate the roof of a luxurious new cabin at Topridge.

Opposite: The complex intersections arising from the Russian cabin's octagonal geometry required log craftsmanship as painstaking as that of a Fabergé egg.

Throughout the 1960s, Mrs. Post returned to Topridge to reenact her rituals of summer as a grande dame, even as advancing age prevented the once tomboyish hostess—who had "thought nothing of carrying a 75-pound guide boat on her back for a portage"[8]—from joining in the outdoor exertions of her guests. She spent her last summer at Topridge in 1971, and, for the first time, did not open the camp in 1972.

After her death in 1973 at age eighty-six, the Marjorie Merriweather Post Foundation donated much of her collection of Native American art to the Smithsonian, and gave Topridge to New York State, which struggled to operate the camp as a conference center. The withdrawal of the camp from the local tax base gave rise to a politics of resentment in which the property was regarded as a problem, not an opportunity, for government and the public.

To the chagrin of preservationists, the state sold the camp at auction in 1985 for $911,000 to a self-described "hot-dog salesman"[9] who was snapping up Adirondack land as "the last nickel bargain in America."[10] When his nickels ran out, his creditors sold Topridge to its current owner, a Texan in search of a summer retreat for his family.

A well-cushioned bench invites an outdoor nap.

After two decades of neglect, Topridge once again bustled with activity. Some buildings were restored, others demolished. A service road—built by the state through miles of forest to allow vehicular access to the camp—was redesigned as a meandering scenic drive to the north side of the lodge, where a porch was built to welcome visitors to a new formal entrance. Richard Giegengack—formerly a partner in the Washington, D.C. office of Skidmore, Owings & Merrill—designed a series of eye-popping new buildings, including a stone chapel and bell tower, and a series of cabins inspired by the traditional woodland architecture of northern Europe.

Just a stone's throw from Mrs. Post's dacha is the most elaborate of them all: a Russian log cabin composed of nine nested octagons, topped by five onion domes. With its traditional log walls wrapped around every modern appointment, including central air conditioning, walk-in closets and heated bathroom floors, the Russian cabin is as fantastic and delightful a piece of scenography as the icy love nest shared by Julie Christie and Omar Sharif in *Dr. Zhivago*.

"We're going to out-Dacha the Dacha,"[11] declared the architect, with what some might regard as effrontery, or, at best, a certain excess of zeal. But Mrs. Post, no stranger herself to the pleasure of gilding an Adirondak lily, might well have recognized a kindred spirit.

Twilight on the north porch of the lodge at Camp Topridge.

WAWAPEK FARM

COLD SPRING HARBOR, NEW YORK

Grosvenor Atterbury

1898–1900

Opposite: The drive to Wawapek leads to an arch that recalls H. H. Richardson's design for the Ames Gate Lodge.

First Overleaf: The entrance court at Wawapek is nestled between the house and the rising hillside. The kitchen was located in the wing to the right of the arch, isolating noise, odors, and the risk of fire from the rest of this summer house.

Second Overleaf: A low ceiling and warm materials make the spacious living hall an invitingly cozy room. Emily de Forest was a noted collector of Early American art and furniture; many of her finest pieces are now in the Metropolitan Museum of Art.

IN 1898 ROBERT AND EMILY DE FOREST asked Grosvenor Atterbury to design a Long Island summer house with the atmosphere of an Adirondack lodge. The architect responded by distilling a variety of motifs—derived from colonial farmhouses, the shingle style, and the artistic camps of the Adirondacks—into a sophisticated work of rustic eclecticism.

The de Forests were pillars of New York society. His ancestors included the first settlers of the Dutch colony of New Amsterdam; her father was a founder of the Metropolitan Museum of Art. At the age of fifty Robert de Forest put aside a lucrative career in corporate law and dedicated himself to philanthropy.[1] This happy transition coincided with the de Forests' decision to build a summer home on land they owned at Cold Spring Harbor. In keeping with the late nineteenth century's nascent interest in Native American culture, they dubbed the property Wawapek Farm, recalling the local Matinecock tribe's description of the area as "a place of good water."[2]

Like many wealthy New Yorkers, the de Forests customarily visited the Adirondacks in the fall. They were members of the Ausable Club, and they visited W. W. Durant at Camp Pine Knot and J. P. Morgan at Camp Uncas. Durant's charming camps probably inspired their desire for a country house with an air of artful rustic comfort.

Grosvenor Atterbury was well acquainted with the latest fashions of both Long Island and the Adirondacks. His father—a law colleague of Robert de Forest—owned a summer home in the Shinnecock Hills, and he belonged to the Tawahus Club in the Adirondacks. Shortly after apprenticing in the office of McKim, Mead & White (Stanford White was another acquaintance of the young architect's father), Atterbury collaborated with W. W. Durant on the design of Camp Uncas, the second of Durant's artistic Adirondack camps.[3]

60

A portrait of Robert de Forest hangs above a teakwood swing designed by his brother, Lockwood de Forest. The dining room lies beyond.

Atterbury placed Wawapek high on a hillside above the eastern shore of Cold Spring Harbor, affording a panoramic view of the water below and the hills of Laurel Hollow beyond. The drive to the house winds uphill to a dramatic entrance arch, much like that of the Ames Gate Lodge. The archway opens into a lovely entrance court, sheltered between the angled wings of the house and the upward slope of the hill. Atterbury's artful conception of this arrival experience suggests that he was familiar with the plans of William Ralph Emerson and other early shingle style architects who considered effects of time, sensation, and emotion as they designed their houses.

The first floor of Wawapek was built of granite, quarried in the Adirondacks, and barged to the beach below the house. A gambrel roof—a form favored by the early Dutch settlers of Long Island—blankets the upper floors. The dominant feature of the courtyard is the elegant screen of columns that fronts the recessed entrance porch and upper balcony. Framed within a broad Dutch gable, this Colonial Revival composition pays architectural homage to the patrician roots of the de Forest family.

The entrance porch opens into a vestibule, which leads directly into the great living hall. The parlor and dining room are located at opposite ends of the living hall. Because the house angles around the curve of the hillside, each room enjoys a different view of the harbor below, and the openings between the rooms create a series of unusual angled interior vistas.

In the central living hall, Atterbury replicated the low, dark, and decidedly masculine mood of the interiors that he had designed with Durant at Camp Uncas, but with finer materials and detailing. In place of logs, the broad ceiling is carried on massive wooden beams. In place of rough siding, the walls are paneled in quarter-sawn oak boards, precisely joined with oversized butterfly joints. The pueblo pots and baskets that ring the cornice were collected during a family tour of the Southwest; the moose over the fireplace lost its head during a hunting trip in Canada.[4]

Atterbury's design of Wawapek led to a series of important commissions arranged by Robert de Forest. Among them were the American Wing of the Metropolitan Museum of Arts (the de Forests were the great benefactors of the wing) and the headquarters of the Russell Sage Foundation (de Forest was president of this charitable foundation). Today Atterbury is best remembered for the design of Forest Hills Gardens, a model suburb sponsored by the Russell Sage Foundation. There his talent for eclectic design was deployed in the creation of housing of unusual solidity and charm for middle class New Yorkers.

*The garden porch. Rustic materials are
combined with Colonial Revival details.*

OLD FAITHFUL INN

YELLOWSTONE NATIONAL PARK, WYOMING

Robert C. Reamer

1903–1904

The lobby is entered through massive doors designed to reassure guests about their safety in the wilderness. A local blacksmith made the wrought iron hinges, coiled doorbell and enormous lock.

Opposite: A towering chimney built of 500 tons of rhyolite rises 85 feet to the ceiling of the lobby. The base of the chimney contains four large hearths and four small corner hearths. A wrought iron and brass clock keeps guests on time for the clockwork eruptions occurring out-of-doors.

Previous overleaf: The porte-cochere is carried on eight sets of dovetailed log cribs, an allusion to railroad trestles that honors the Northern Pacific Railroad's role in building the Old Faithful Inn.

You sleep in a room with log walls, where the electric juice responds to your touch, hot water flows from the faucet, and a bebuttoned bellboy answers your call.

F. Dumont Smith, *Book of a Hundred Bears*, 1909

W HEN THE NORTHERN PACIFIC RAILROAD initiated rail service to Yellowstone National Park in 1883, the number of visitors to the park jumped from 1,000 to 5,000 in one year.[1] As Yellowstone became a popular tourist destination, the Northern Pacific took an interest in the development of facilities that would appeal to its well-heeled passengers.

Primitive lodgings like Yancey's Hotel—where a guest might find a clean bed "when there are sheets enough to go around"[2]—were supplanted by comfortable, if nondescript, hotels near some of Yellowstone's most appealing scenery: Mammoth Hot Springs, Lake Yellowstone, the Grand Canyon, and the Lower Geyser Basin.

After the failure of several attempts to build a similar hotel near the Old Faithful geyser, the Northern Pacific reorganized Yellowstone's hotel operations under the leadership of Harry Child, a Montana businessman. In early 1903, Child had already begun planning a series of log cabins overlooking Old Faithful when he met Robert Reamer, a young California architect, while vacationing at the Hotel del Coronado. Soon the two men were on a train heading east, with Child explaining "he wanted something unique and appropriate"[3] while Reamer made preliminary sketches of a rustic hotel resembling a wildly overscaled Adirondack lodge.

When the Old Faithful Inn opened on June 1, 1904, it was a sensation. Guests encountered a building of boulders and logs beneath a great sloping roof, which offered the vicarious experience of staying in a frontiersman's cabin. Indeed, like a cabin on the vanished frontier, the inn was literally built from the land around it: lodgepole pines from Yellowstone's great forests were hauled to the construction site; rhyolite, a lava rock produced by the volcanic explosions that created Yellowstone's caldera, was quarried just a few miles away.

Above: The Crow's Nest is a fanciful tree house located just beneath the peak of the ceiling. Musicians once played from this perch, as guests danced far below.

As in many rustic buildings, the true glory of the Old Faithful Inn lies within, in its soaring lobby. While hotels with vast interior spaces were hardly unknown in the West—both the Palace Hotel in San Francisco and Denver's Brown Palace were built around roofed courtyards—the Old Faithful Inn was the first hotel to reinterpret such a space with a rustic aesthetic, in which natural materials are at once structural and decorative, functional and whimsical. Much as Durant had done at Camp Pine Knot, Reamer gathered deformed branches and gnarled logs to use as railings and balusters, and even the lobby's drinking fountain was subject to rustic reinterpretation: it was carved from a block of rhyolite.

Opposite: Balconies and bridges fill the upper reaches of the lobby like the branches of a forest. The lobby bore an even stronger resemblance to a forest before 1940, when its lodgepole pines were stripped of their bark. Some aesthetic recompense was found in the revelation of intricate patterns carved by pine bark beetles.

75

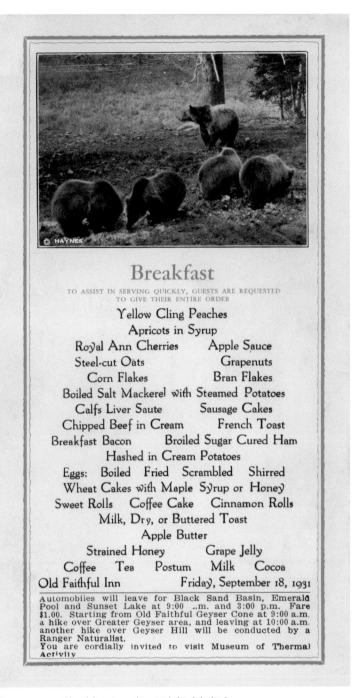

Breakfast

TO ASSIST IN SERVING QUICKLY, GUESTS ARE REQUESTED
TO GIVE THEIR ENTIRE ORDER

Yellow Cling Peaches

Apricots in Syrup

Royal Ann Cherries   Apple Sauce

Steel-cut Oats   Grapenuts

Corn Flakes   Bran Flakes

Boiled Salt Mackerel with Steamed Potatoes

Calfs Liver Saute   Sausage Cakes

Chipped Beef in Cream   French Toast

Breakfast Bacon   Broiled Sugar Cured Ham

Hashed in Cream Potatoes

Eggs: Boiled Fried Scrambled Shirred

Wheat Cakes with Maple Syrup or Honey

Sweet Rolls   Coffee Cake   Cinnamon Rolls

Milk, Dry, or Buttered Toast

Apple Butter

Strained Honey   Grape Jelly

Coffee   Tea   Postum   Milk   Cocoa

Old Faithful Inn   Friday, September 18, 1931

Automobiles will leave for Black Sand Basin, Emerald
Pool and Sunset Lake at 9:00 ..m. and 3:00 p.m. Fare
$1.00. Starting from Old Faithful Geyser Cone at 9:00 a.m.
a hike over Greater Geyser area, and leaving at 10:00 a.m.
another hike over Geyser Hill will be conducted by a
Ranger Naturalist.
You are cordially invited to visit Museum of Thermal
Activity

Bears were served breakfast at a garbage pit behind the kitchen.

Left: The dining room is furnished with its original Old Hickory chairs.

No. 167 BED ROOM OLD FAITHFUL INN—YELLOWSTONE PARK.   HAYNES-PHOTO.   Printed in Germany.

Along with its architectural evocations of frontier cabins and primeval forests, the Old Faithful Inn offered all the comforts and conveniences of a fine resort hotel. It was among the first generation of American hotels with extensive electric lighting; and while the building was never intended for anything other than summer occupancy, it was nonetheless equipped with steam heat to ward off the frequently chilly nights of summer at an elevation exceeding 7,000 feet.

Reamer decorated the public spaces of the inn with Native American rugs and handsome Arts & Crafts furniture designed and manufactured by Charles Limbert, a lesser-known but worthy contemporary of Gustav Stickley. The animal trophies and bearskin rugs that are nearly ubiquitous in the lodges of the Adirondacks and other mountain resorts are nowhere to be found at the Old Faithful Inn, because hunting has never been permitted within Yellowstone National Park.

The Old Faithful Inn was so widely acclaimed in railroad advertising that it became the best-known rustic building in America, a familiar image even to those who had never traveled to Yellowstone. To promote its service to Yellowstone's western entrance, the Union Pacific went so far as to build a full-scale replica of the inn at the 1915 Panama–Pacific International Exposition in San Francisco.[4]

The influence of Robert Reamer's superb example of architecture in harmony with nature was echoed in many later park hotels, including the Ahwahnee at Yosemite and Timberline Lodge on Mount Hood. The result was a democratization of rustic architecture: while wealthy Easterners had their Adirondack camps, Midwesterners their Great Lake retreats, and Westerners their mysterious Bohemian Grove,[5] upper-middle-class Americans could enjoy the same outdoor exertions and indoor delights by checking into an artful rustic hotel.

Opposite: Stair treads were made of half-logs; gnarled branches were fashioned into balusters.

Overleaf: The Old Faithful Inn has become as much an icon of Yellowstone National Park as the geyser itself.

CHARLES MILLARD PRATT HOUSE

OJAI, CALIFORNIA

Greene & Greene

1909–1911

84

In a corner of the front terrace, an artful collage of native boulders, clinker bricks, and shingles recalls the vigorous use of natural materials by Henry Hobson Richardson and William Ralph Emerson.

CHARLES AND MARY PRATT were among the first of many wealthy Easterners drawn to the rugged beauty and Mediterranean climate of the Ojai Valley. In 1908 the Pratts asked the brothers Charles and Henry Greene to design their winter home on a ridge overlooking the valley. The resulting low-slung and rambling lodge is a rustic version of the famed Arts & Crafts mansions—"the ultimate bungalows"[1]—that the Greenes designed for suburban plots in Pasadena.

Charles Millard Pratt was a second generation oil tycoon. His father—the developer of a kerosene sold with the slogan "the holy lamps of Tibet are primed with Astral Oil"[2]—merged his refineries with those of John D. Rockefeller in 1874, thus becoming a founding partner of the Standard Oil conglomerate. When his father died in 1891, Pratt assumed many of his responsibilities, overseeing his investments and philanthropic enterprises, while serving variously as a director, secretary, and treasurer of "the Standard."

Pratt also inherited his father's tastes for informal family vacations and for rustic architecture. In 1870 the elder Pratt had built one of the first permanent camps in the Adirondacks, a "hewn log structure of rustic design"[3] constructed by local guides. In 1909 Charles and Mary Pratt established their own modest camp at Little Moose Lake, within the vast preserve of the Adirondack League. Designed by Buffalo architect William S. Wicks, the camp's several cottages were linked by covered walkways; within were rooms joined by broad doorways, their woodsy interiors lit by many windows.[4] The Pratt summer home on Long Island was similarly unpretentious. Clad entirely in shingles, it was designed in 1890 by Charles Alonzo Rich, who had worked as William Ralph Emerson's draftsman in the late 1870s,[5] when Emerson was designing several of the early masterpieces of the emerging Shingle Style.

Preceding Overleaf: The Pratt House rambles across terraces and foundation walls built of native boulders. The varied rooflines of the house echo the shapes of the nearby mountains.

Opposite: The slightly upturned roof ends were a Japanese-inspired accent favored by the Greene brothers.

Following overleaf: As in many Shingle Style designs, the hall serves as both the living room and circulation hub of the house. The built-in bench by the fireplace establishes a cozy retreat within the larger space.

A stylized oak branch decorates an interior window of iridescent glass

Opposite: The soaring height of the small dining room makes a dramatic spatial contrast to the low-ceilinged rooms throughout the rest of the house. The octagonal chandelier is decorated with rubies and jade from the gem collection of Mary Pratt. The chevron patterning of the fireplace bricks was derived from Native American textiles.

Following overleaf: On the rear terrace, Japanese-inspired timberwork supports an upper deck. The living space of the house is nearly doubled by its terraces, decks and sleeping porches.

In Ojai, the Pratts preferred to entertain at the nearby Foothills Hotel, and to live casually at home. Accordingly, the Greene brothers designed their house without large spaces for entertaining and extensive service quarters. The plan resembles a flattened U, with two asymmetrical wings opening broadly to a rear terrace and a view of the foothills. The taller wing contains two levels of bedrooms; the lower wing contains the dining room, pantry, and kitchen. Located at the bend of the U, the living hall is an expansive, low-ceilinged space that serves as an entrance hall, reception room, and living room all rolled into one. As a consequence of this elongated plan, most of the house is only one room deep and nearly all the rooms have windows that look to both sides of the house. Shifting patterns of sunlight and shadow dance through the rooms from dawn until dusk, emphasizing the home's connection to the garden just outside, and to the natural world beyond.

The design strategies that Charles and Henry Greene employed in commissions like the Pratt House were rooted in their youthful experiences in late-nineteenth-century Boston.[6] Charles and Henry completed two years of formal architectural education at MIT in 1890, and then worked as apprentices to some of Boston's leading architects—many of them protégés of the recently deceased Henry Hobson Richardson—before establishing the office of Greene & Greene of Pasadena in 1893.

Charles was a talented watercolorist, and his painting excursions along the North Shore of Boston acquainted him with the shingled vacation houses that had arisen there in the 1880s, including several designed by William Ralph Emerson. The architectural historian Pamela Fox[7] has speculated that the Greene brothers' use of shouldered beams—as in the living hall of the Pratt House—may attest to their knowledge of the curious beams in the dining room of the Loring House (see page 17). In any event, the Greene brothers were exposed at the beginning of their careers to buildings with informal plans, a clear expression of structure, and a bold use of natural materials.

Boston was also the acknowledged center of Japanese scholarship, and the brothers' interest in Japanese design was awakened during their five years in the city. The influence of Japanese architecture became apparent in the brothers' designs after 1903, when Charles purchased a copy of *Japanese Homes and their Surroundings*, Edward S. Morse's definitive book on the topic. In later years Charles credited Morse's illustrations with helping the brothers develop the mature style of their ultimate bungalows,[8] which emphasized an artistic expression of post and beam construction, and the unification of house and garden as a setting for informal living.

THE POINT
(*formerly* CAMP WONUNDRA)

SARANAC LAKE, NEW YORK

William G. Distin

1931–1933

An octagonal entrance vestibule is nestled between two wings of the lodge. William Distin's inspiration for the angled layout of the lodge may well have come from the Shingle Style houses of William Ralph Emerson, which Distin studied in his sketchbooks.

Preceding overleaf: Camp Wonundra's boathouse was designed as a streamlined updating of traditional Adirondack boat houses, with geometric patterns replacing naturalistic decorations.

Opposite: The walls and ceilings of the lodge are sleekly paneled in wide pine boards.

Following overleaf: The living hall at the center of the lodge was also used as the camp's dining room.

THE FOLLOWING STORY concerning the architect William Distin has become a familiar chestnut of Adirondack lore:

> Distin was told by a New York client, after approval of a camp design, "I'm leaving for Europe. I want it built and finished the day I return." As the camp neared completion, the owner cabled: "Will arrive Thursday. Please buy dishes and have roast lamb for dinner." The owner arrived, and china, silver, flowers and roast lamb were on the table.[1]

Distin's training in the care and feeding of wealthy clients began in 1900, when he entered the office of William Coulter as a sixteen-year-old apprentice. Coulter was the Adirondacks' first professional architect and a prodigious designer of grandly scaled rustic camps. As Distin gained experience and poise, Coulter gave him greater responsibility in designing camps and overseeing their construction. After Coulter's death in 1907, Distin attended Columbia University and earned a professional degree in architecture. He returned to Saranac Lake after World War I and established his own practice in 1921.

In the 1920s the Adirondacks were slowly falling out of fashion as a summer resort; the Depression and World War II accelerated this fall. With wealthy clients for private camps few and far between, Distin designed churches, schools, banks, hotels, and, most notably, the vast ice arena for the 1932 Olympic Games in Lake Placid. Still, a handful of clients came his way with rustic commissions, and these resulted in the construction of the last of the luxurious camps of the Adirondacks.

One such client was William Avery Rockefeller II, a grandnephew of the founder of Standard Oil. Rockefeller was between marriages in 1931, and perhaps suffering from his very own depression, when he commissioned Distin to design a camp for year-round use on a rocky peninsula in Upper Saranac Lake.

The master bedroom is brightened by windows in its opposite walls.

Steel casement windows—with steam radiators beneath—give a decidedly modern flavor to the rustic architecture of Camp Wonundra.

Wonundra means "big rock" in the language of Australian aborigines, and Distin turned the rock-strewn forest setting to expressive advantage in designing the camp. Buildings are rooted to the ground by massive foundations made of native stone. Stone terraces extend rooms into the out-of-doors, where towering old pines stood in the way; the terraces were built around them.

Camp Wonundra is comprised of only three major buildings: the main lodge, a sizable guest cabin with additional bedrooms, and the boathouse. Each building was sited to offer superb views of the lake, the far shorelines and the distant mountains. No attempt was made to connect the widely separated buildings, except for meandering walkways made of large stones pulled from the site. Even a comfortable stroll around the camp retains some of the feeling of scrambling over rocks.

The lodge is the most impressive of the buildings. Above stone foundations, frame walls are clad with enormous horizontal half-logs, some as large as two feet in diameter. Corners are detailed with projecting whole logs, maintaining the illusion of true log construction. The chalet-like gables are covered with vertical half-logs; stepped projections of horizontal logs appear to support the eaves. These motifs can be traced back to W. W. Durant.[2] Ironically, Distin had to import logs for Camp Wonundra from Canada, because nineteenth-century loggers had felled nearly all of the Adirondacks' first growth trees.

The lodge is composed of three wings radiating from a grand living hall. Family bedrooms are in one wing, guest bedrooms in the opposite wing. A service wing is connected to the west end of the great hall, away from the lake. Distin adjusted this plan to the terrain by raising the family bedrooms a half level above the living hall, and lowering the guest rooms a few steps below it.

The interior of the lodge has an air of streamlined elegance, reminding us that Camp Wonundra was indeed a creation of the forward-looking architecture of the 1930s. Distin did very little just for decorative effect; instead he relied on elegant materials and a direct expression of structure to create visual interest. In the living hall, the wide pegged floors and the horizontal paneling of the walls and ceiling establish a calm, ordered background. Against this background the dynamic elements of the room—the twin fireplaces, the muscular trusses, the gilt-framed paintings and animal trophy heads—stand in dramatic relief.

The bedrooms of the lodge were designed for comfort and repose. Simple paneling and broad expanses of windows emphasize their generous dimensions. While each room is centered on a traditional fireplace, modern steam radiators are hidden beneath the metal casement windows. Vast walk-in closets afford ample storage for guests making lengthy visits and prevent sound from traveling room to room. Bathrooms are the epitome of 1930s luxe moderne; they appear to have wandered away from Central Park West and gotten lost in the woods. If any camp in the Adirondacks might be classified as Rustic Deco, Wonundra is it.

Rockefeller sold Camp Wonundra in 1969, and after a quick succession of several owners it was acquired by David and Christie Garrett in 1986. The Garretts transformed the camp into The Point, a unique small resort. Guests at The Point are encouraged to feel that they've been invited to their rich uncle's camp for a rustic house party. Nearly all of them surrender to this fantasy upon arrival, when they are greeted with champagne and a grand tour of the property. If William Distin were to see them at the end of the day, as they sit down to dinner around a table set with china, silver, and flowers, he would surely be pleased.

Opposite: Beautifully tiled bathrooms were the last word in 1930s luxury.

Following overleaf: Broad overhangs, bold log work and expansive red windows recall the early Adirondack architecture of the Swiss Cottage at Camp Pine Knot.

102

FALLINGWATER

MILL RUN, PENNSYLVANIA

Frank Lloyd Wright

1935–39

FALLINGWATER, a weekend house designed by Frank Lloyd Wright for Pittsburgh department store magnate E. J. Kaufmann and his family, is so well-known and so well-loved as a master-piece of modern architecture that our brief visit may well bene-fit from an introduction comprising a few coolly descriptive statements:

- *This is the country house of a wealthy urban family.*
- *The architect fit the house to its setting with sensitivity and imagination.*
- *Local material was used in building the house, connecting it to nature.*
- *Large windows open the house to sunlight and the natural world.*

Curiously, these statements, which describe Fallingwater to a proverbial T, are drawn directly from an account of the Shingle Style houses that William Ralph Emerson designed in Maine and Massachusetts between 1879 and 1886.[1] The fact that such de-scriptions apply equally well to Fallingwater above the falls of Bear Run and to the Loring House overlooking Plum Cove (pages 10-21) suggests that Wright's modern masterpiece may not have suddenly sprung *sui generis* from the architect's imagination, but that it arose from his knowledge of a tradition in the design of houses for natural settings.

The architectural historian Vincent Scully, a fervent but dis-cerning admirer of Wright's work, was among the first to connect the architect's innovative houses to an American past. In his now-classic study, *The Shingle Style and the Stick Style: Architectural Theory and Design from Downing to the Origins of Wright*, Scully takes note of some essential qualities of the Shingle Style that appear and reappear—well assimilated, but identifiable all the same—in Wright's cele-brated Prairie Houses of 1900-1909:

- *Masses are coherently interwoven.*
- *Open plans are clearly organized.*
- *Interiors flow outward to exterior porches.*
- *Eclectic cultural references are synthesized into an original whole.*[2]

The hearth of the living room fireplace is a boulder that rises through the flagstone floor. A chestnut stump serves as a rustic bar.

While Scully concludes his chapter on Wright with his discussion of the Prairie Houses, one can easily skip forward in time to include Fallingwater, which exemplifies so many of the characteristics of form and space that Wright had assimilated from the Shingle Style: a coherent interweaving of masses appears in the crossing of the two major balconies, which balance the soaring stone tower; a clearly organized open plan occurs in the division of the living-dining room into discreet areas for a variety of social activities; the compact interior space of the house is nearly doubled by its balconies and terraces; the low ceilings and broad fireplace recall dwellings on the colonial frontier.

Wright's reliance on innovations rooted in the 1880s and his frequent allusions to history led to Philip Johnson's quip (circa 1932-33) that Wright was "the greatest architect of the nineteenth century."[3] This was a blow upon a bruise already suffered by Wright: after attempting to exclude Wright altogether, Johnson and Henry Russell-Hitchcock had only grudgingly included him in the Museum of Modern Art's influential *Modern Architecture: International Exhibition*, while lavishing attention on the International Style modernism of Walter Gropius, Mies van der Rohe, and Le Corbusier.

Wright saw Fallingwater as his opportunity "to beat the Internationalists at their own game"[4] and reassert his preeminence in his profession. For the first time in his career, he designed a house as abstract as a cubist sculpture, with no decoration save for the patterning of its sandstone piers and walls. The stone was quarried from the site and laid up in narrow courses with rugged edges, a treatment inspired by the eroded cliffs along Bear Run.

In contrast to the rugged sandstone, the concrete balconies and terraces have rounded corners, giving them an unusually weighty presence that distinguishes them from the crisp concrete work of most International Style buildings. As the horizontal layers of Fallingwater descend into Bear Run, their bright surfaces and deep shadows evoke the stratified geology of the ravine itself.

Wright's ability to conjure abstractions of such natural phenomena has been persuasively credited to his knowledge of Japanese prints, "in which natural forms were transformed through knowledge and love into another medium, without being killed through imitation."[5] His success in transforming nature into a man-made structure that deepens man's connection to nature has made Fallingwater an inspiration for architects seeking to design modern homes in harmony with the natural world.

A Sung Dynasty cast-iron Buddha evokes Frank Lloyd Wright's affinity for the arts of the Far East.

Opposite: Traditional peasant chairs from Italy join Wright's built-in furniture in the dining corner of the living room. With its low ceiling, broad fireplace, lord-of-the-manor portrait and Indian baskets, this room makes for an interesting comparison with the living room of Wawapek Farm (pages 60-69).

FORTUNE ROCK

MOUNT DESERT ISLAND, MAINE

George Howe

1937–1939

The framing of Fortune Rock was painted black and covered with panels of plywood separated by slender reveals. As in many traditional cottages along the Maine Coast, no plaster was used in the house.

Preceding overleaf: George Howe's design for Fortune Rock was influenced by his memories of simple childhood summers on Mount Desert Island.

Opposite: The wide stair to the living room accommodated Clara Fargo Thomas' love of dramatic entrances when she entertained.

Following overleaf: The living room appears to float above the sea. The glossy blue paint of the wooden ceiling extends out to the eaves, further blurring the boundaries of indoors and out.

C LARA FARGO THOMAS cut an unusual figure in 1930s society in New York. She was an heiress, the wife of a well-known sportsman, and the mother of two children; she was also an accomplished muralist with a booming career. She had begun by decorating her son's nursery, then the walls of her friends' houses and offices. Equal to any challenge, she was soon supervising corporate commissions and a team of assistants.

As a child, Thomas had summered in the Adirondacks; she recalled "the open feeling of a tent with only mosquito netting between her and nature."[1] In 1937, when she began planning her summer home on the resort island of Mount Desert, she turned to George Howe for the design of a contemporary home with a similarly open quality.

Howe was a fervent convert to modernism. After a decade of discontent as a partner in Mellor, Meigs and Howe of Philadelphia, he announced in 1928 that he had designed his last "Jumbo, Anti-Economy Romantic Country House package."[2] He formed a new partnership with William Lescaze, a young Swiss modernist, and designed the headquarters of the Philadelphia Savings Fund Society. When the building opened in 1932 it was hailed as America's first truly modern skyscraper.

Howe knew Mount Desert well—as a student at Groton, he had spent summers at his mother's Shingle Style cottage at Northeast Harbor. Howe and Thomas reconnoitered the island together, and they chose a ledge of pink granite above Somes Sound as the site of Fortune Rock.

Howe devised a simple plan: the entrance, kitchen, dining room, and bedrooms comprised a long wing at the edge of the granite ledge; the living room was set a half-level below. Thomas wanted the living room to extend over the water as far as possible, so Howe designed the dramatic cantilever that carries it.

The rooms of Fortune Rock are flooded with light even during inclement weather. Mrs. Thomas' bedroom once held built-in furniture made by Wharton Esherick.

Inside, the living room hovers magically between sea and sky. The glossy blue ceiling extends out to the edge of the eaves; the header beams are concealed above the ceiling joists. When sun hits the water, sparkling reflections ripple across the ceiling, producing the thrilling sensation that one is swimming in the room.

Fortune Rock was built with the traditional materials of coastal Maine. The roof was clad with cedar shingles, the outer walls with oiled cedar clapboards. Ceilings were planked, interior walls paneled with plywood. No plaster was used; Thomas' son recalled, "It had an innate formality that did not fit mother's Maine mood. Her attitude was exemplified by her preference for a rough dirt driveway and her slight feeling of reverse snobbism toward people who anxiously ventured to come visit her in their luxurious city cars."[3]

Howe's plans for the site included an owner's cottage, a children's cottage, a boathouse, and a floating dock; Thomas imagined that the house would ultimately function as a central gathering place, much like the lodge of an Adirondack camp. World War II stalled these plans, and the house was left to stand in splendid isolation above the rocky shore.

Clara Fargo Thomas died in 1970, and the property was sold to a family from Philadelphia. They restored the house and redecorated it with a new, understated elegance. Today, Fortune Rock survives as both an icon of early modernism, and as a well-loved summer home.

Opposite: This narrow corridor runs along the inland length of the house, so that no room is blocked from a view of the water.

Following overleaf: Fortune Rock overlooks the length of Somes Sound.

WHARTON ESHERICK'S STUDIO

PAOLI, PENNSYLVANIA

1926–1966

Such a studio built by the craftsman's own hands out of chunks of rock and great balks of timber, sinking back into the quiet woods on a quiet crag with, below its long windows, quiet fields parceled out by the string-courses of hedges and running to a quietly rising horizon … such a quiet spot is the best place to think in.

Ford Madox Ford, *Great Trade Route*, 1937

Wharton Esherick was born into a prosperous Philadelphia family in 1887. To their dismay, he eschewed a career in commerce for a life of self-expression in the arts. He took courses in woodworking and metalsmithing at the Manual Training High School and then studied painting at the Philadelphia School of Industrial Art. He received a scholarship to the Philadelphia Academy of Fine Arts, but the Academy's fusty traditionalism was so alien to him that he quit the school just before graduating. He then began working as an illustrator by day while struggling to paint like an Impressionist at night.

After reading Thoreau's *Walden*, Esherick bought a derelict farm on a wooded slope above the village of Paoli, and moved to the country for good in 1913. While savoring his new life in the woods, he continued to struggle as a painter. Frustration and hardship gradually led him to other forms of expression. He learned the craft of carving and printing woodblocks, and produced prints that appeared in magazines, including *Century* and *Vanity Fair*, and in limited-edition books. He also began using his chisels to redecorate Victorian furniture that he disliked, and to carve decorative frames for his paintings.

After struggling for twenty years as a painter, Esherick saw the light when his picture frames aroused more interest than the paintings they contained and when an admiring neighbor offered to buy the family dining table that he had just built. In 1924

Opposite: The studio's stucco tower was daubed with paint in a suggestion of dappled sunlight.

Following overleaf: Esherick's celebrated tree-like staircase rises from the studio mezzanine to the sculptor's bedroom, with a mid-level branch reaching to the kitchen. Whimsical garden horses once grazed the grounds around the studio.

120

he quit painting for good, declaring, "If I can't paint like Esherick, I can at least sculpt like Esherick."[1] At the age of 37, he reinvented himself as a sculptor and furniture designer, a choice that led, in the end, to acclaim for the "Dean of American Craftsman" and a small measure of material success.

In 1926 Esherick began building a studio for his new work on a ridge above the old farmhouse. The studio evolved over the next four decades, and came to resemble a cubist collage of stone, board-and-batten siding, and stucco, all common materials of the farm buildings in the valley below.

The studio was built on two levels, with a day-lit mezzanine looking down into a well. One of Esherick's consummate works, a stair of spiraling slabs of red oak, rises to his bedroom. Alert to every opportunity for craftsmanship, Esherick made nearly all the contents of his studio himself, even down to light switches fashioned from oxtail bones. The studio represents such a complete rejection of mass-produced goods that a visitor may be startled by the banal presence of a vintage Western Electric Model 500 telephone.

During the 1930s Esherick received a number of commissions from Philadelphia's Main Line gentry. The most elaborate began with an order for bookshelves and ended in the complete renovation of Curtis Bok's mansion in Gulph Mills, which Esherick outfitted with exquisitely crafted Deco doorframes and mantels, and a sweeping spiral stair.

The Bok commission inspired architect George Howe to invite Esherick to collaborate in designing a "Pennsylvania Hill House" for the "America at Home" pavilion at the 1939-1940 World's Fair. Esherick used boards milled from a cherry tree at Paoli for the paneling of Howe's "summer camp"[2] and furnished it with a table and "handmade chairs of slender finished hickory with stretched parchment seats like drum-heads [that] are lightweight and comfortable and follow the best crafts tradition."[3] The critic Talbot Hamlin praised this ensemble: "The joy of making things for one's self is a very real satisfaction; and when this is joined to that creative imagination in the handling of wood … which runs through this room … the result is not only beautiful but eminently timeless."[4]

Sadly, neither of these important commissions proved to be timeless. The "Pennsylvania Hill House" was dismantled with the rest of the World's Fair, and the Bok residence was demolished in 1989. Fate has been much kinder to Esherick's ultimate masterpiece: since his death in 1970, the Wharton Esherick Museum has maintained his studio and its collections intact, and has welcomed visitors to one of the world's most delightfully eccentric house-museums.

A simian gymnast gives life to Esherick's credo: "If it isn't fun, it isn't worth doing."

Opposite: Esherick's loft bedroom contains work from every stage of his career: drawings, paintings, cubist sculpture, and the sensuous furniture of his mature style.

A ceramic pelican adorns a terrace leading to the studio. The unusually shaped columns were inspired by those found on traditional Pennsylvania barns, which were gradually deformed by the cows that habitually rubbed against them.

Left: Esherick's studio complex grew more abstract with each addition. The workshop building to the right was designed by Louis Kahn in 1955.

MANITOGA

GARRISON, NEW YORK

Russel Wright & David Leavitt

1942–1976

Large windows and rugged materials dissolve the boundaries of indoors and out.

From the 1930s through the 1950s, Russel Wright was America's best-known industrial designer. The success of his designs (including the production of over 250 million pieces of American Modern dinnerware stamped with his distinctive signature) and his many prescriptions for a domestic life of informal comfort and convenience (most notably in his bestselling *Guide to Easier Living*) made him the first lifestyle celebrity.

Wright's wife, Mary Small Einstein, was the business genius behind the Russel Wright brand. Born into a wealthy New York family—her father was a manufacturer of rugs and draperies—Mary Wright applied her formidable talents for marketing and promotion to her husband's work.

In 1939 the Wrights took a cross-country trip to California, where they admired modernist houses designed by Harwell Hamilton Harris and Richard Neutra. The Wrights were so taken with the concept of casual, outdoor living that they pondered relocating to California; but they soon settled on the more practical course of finding a weekend retreat near New York City. In 1941 they bought a weathered cottage on eighty acres in the Hudson Highlands, near the town of Garrison.

The property that Wright would call Manitoga—after an Algonquin word meaning "place of the great spirit"—had been ravaged by logging and quarrying. A dense second-growth forest had sprung up around the cottage, depriving it of light and air. Wright first thinned the trees around the cottage, and then took to restoring the natural beauty of ever-larger areas of the woods beyond. He created a waterfall and a pond for swimming by redirecting a stream into the largest of the old quarry pits, and he laid out paths linking woodland rooms filled with masses of indigenous flora—laurel, ferns, mosses—that he created by cultivating some plants and culling others.

When Mary Wright died of breast cancer in 1952, Russel was left to raise their two-year old adopted daughter, Ann, as a widower. Always a homebody, he gradually withdrew from his design practice in New York and devoted more and more time to Ann and to developing the landscape of Manitoga.

In 1955 Wright traveled to Asia as a State Department development consultant. In Japan, he visited the stroll gardens of Kyoto, and the Tokyo home of Antonin Raymond, a Czech-American architect who, after working for Frank Lloyd Wright during the construction of the Imperial Hotel, had established his own reputation as an innovative synthesizer of traditional Japanese forms with the modern architecture of the West.

A shower like a waterfall.

The bathroom opens to a private terrace with an outdoor fireplace.

A continuous band of windows runs around the studio.

Shelving and curtains demarcate Wright's bedroom within his open-plan studio.

Soon after his return from Japan, Wright contacted David Leavitt, a young New York architect who had worked for Raymond in Tokyo, and engaged him to collaborate in the design of a Japanese-influenced modernist home at Manitoga, in keeping with Wright's wish that "the shape of the quarry and the surrounding contours of the land and the rocks must always be visually the most important part of the scene."[1] To honor young Ann Wright's observation that the rock forms of the quarry's southern face resembled a great dragon drinking from the pond, the new home was named Dragon Rock.

Dragon Rock is composed of two buildings of unequal size, linked by a pergola. Within the larger building, the public areas of the home—entry hall, living and dining areas, kitchen, and den—are arranged on a series of split-levels. This arrangement, so suggestive of climbing in a quarry, creates a rich variety of interior and exterior views.

In the living and dining areas, nature is brought boldly indoors: boulders of Richardsonian size are piled to form stairs and fireplaces, a tree trunk supports the roof, expansive walls of glass provide only a nominal sense of enclosure. One of Ann's friends related that "being in Ann's house is a little like camping out—except that everything is comfortable."[2]

Ann and her governess occupied rooms at the far end of the building. These rooms—along with a bathroom equipped with a waterfall for a shower and a tree branch for a coat rack—open to a terrace with an outdoor fireplace, set into a great pile of stones that resembles the head of King Kong.

Dragon Rock's smaller building holds Wright's studio, a guest room, and a bathroom. Wright placed his bedroom in a corner of the studio, and screened it with bookshelves and a floor-to-ceiling curtain. Even this spartan setting is graced with rustic details: the bath paneling is cedar, the guest bedroom's door is veneered in a continuous sheet of birch bark (a modernist take on rustic tradition) and the window shades are decorated with Wright's delicate drawings of ferns.

Wright closed his New York studio in 1965 and devoted himself to Manitoga, which he hoped would survive him as a nature sanctuary. When he died in 1976, he had completely revitalized the woods and built eleven pathways—each a carefully orchestrated sequence of sights and sensations—with a total length of four miles.

If Manitoga offers ample evidence of Wright's interest in Japanese influences, particularly the stroll garden, it also testifies to the lasting power of the picturesque aesthetic of that native son of the Hudson valley, Andrew Jackson Downing. Wright's descriptions of his woodland paths echo with Downing's account of the delight he took in the wilderness of Montgomery Place, just fifty miles upriver from Manitoga:

"A richly wooded and highly picturesque valley, filled with the richest growth of trees, and threaded with dark, intricate, and mazy walks . . ."[3]

Manitoga is home to the Russel Wright Design Center. The grounds are open to the public; tours of Dragon Rock are available by appointment.

Opposite: Wright established plantings on the roofs of Dragon Rock, to more completely meld buildings and landscape.

ROLAND TERRY'S HOUSE

LOPEZ ISLAND, WASHINGTON

Roland Terry

1959–1963

Above: The elegantly informal living room.

Preceding overleaf: Terry's studio (left) and house (right) overlook the Strait of Juan de Fuca.

The San Juan Islands are blessed with fair weather, thanks to their location within the rain shadow of the Olympic Peninsula. Although the islands lie just a hundred miles north of Seattle, they receive only half that city's rainfall, a happy quirk of geography that has long attracted refugees from the soggy mainland. On Lopez Island—the most pastoral of the islands—cacti grow in profusion along its southern coast, and it was here that Terry built his celebrated weekend home.

The late Roland Terry was a Seattle architect who played a prominent role in developing a Northwestern style of modern architecture after World War II. The houses that he designed in the 1950s and 1960s are now cherished as icons of an era when Seattle was a sophisticated but small city. Jim Olson, a partner in the Seattle firm of Olson Sundberg Kundig Allen, has recalled Terry's career in superlatives:

> Roland Terry was the man. For residential design at the highest of the high end, no one else came close. He created an environment, a lifestyle, with a sense of history. It was a very cosmopolitan kind of thing. He was like a high-end interior designer, but also an architect, and so was able to create warm, comfortable, yet architectural environments. I can't think of anyone else who did what he did, wedding European elegance with Northwest Modernism.[1]

Terry studied architecture during the late 1930s at the University of Washington. Two teachers were particularly influential: the architect Lionel Pries and the interior designer Hope Foote. Pries had studied under John Galen Howard at the University of California at Berkeley and under Paul Cret at the University of Pennsylvania. Howard and Cret were both graduates of the École des Beaux-Arts, and they modeled their own teaching on the classical precepts of the École.

At a time when International Style modernism exerted increasing influence on American architecture, Pries asserted the continuing value of the Beaux-Arts tradition of logical, hierarchical planning to his students. Pries also opened their eyes "to a larger world, which encompassed foreign travel, classical music, art history, crafts, and fine arts as well as architecture."[2] Terry recalled that Pries "made great sketches, and he knew what he was drawing. He thought designers should make complete buildings, with the inside and outside linked and integrated."[3]

Hope Foote led one of the first university-level interior design programs. She was an inventor of the "Northwest look" that made extensive use of natural wood, stone, and native plantings. She substituted architectural built-ins for conventional furniture and grouped seating in the middle of rooms to encourage conversation.

By the 1950s Terry was an established designer of well-planned and suavely detailed houses in Seattle. He also designed a very rugged house for the John Day family on their ranch overlooking Oregon's Rogue River Valley. Large windows were set between piers of stone; stone floors flowed outside and became exterior terraces. In the living room the ceiling was carried on deep cedar beams, and the pine-paneled walls were hung with trophy mounts, including a menacing polar bear. This updated version of a rustic lodge provided a stylish home for Mike the cheetah, the Days' outsized house cat.[4]

Terry took a very gentle approach in the planning of his retreat on Lopez Island. He later recalled that,

> This was such a magnificent piece of property that it shouldn't have anything built on it at all. It should have been left in a completely natural state. With that in mind, I made a point of building the house without cutting down any trees, and designed it to intrude on the landscape as little as possible.[5]

This deferential treatment can be felt even before Terry's compound comes into view: a narrow dirt road winds downhill through woodlands, ending in a grass parking court bounded by rock outcroppings and thick hedges. A tall wooden gate beckons.

The gate opens to a lovely inner courtyard, bounded by Terry's architectural studio on one side and a linear water garden on the other. The sight and sound of water are subtle hints of luxury in this semi-arid setting. At the far end of the courtyard, another gate beckons.

The second gate opens to a broad lawn leading from Terry's studio to his house; the two buildings frame a stunning view of the Strait of Juan de Fuca, with the snowy mountains of the Olympic Peninsula as a distant backdrop.

The lower floor of the house was carved into the rocky earth. Terry created a wine cellar with terra cotta drainage pipes.

Opposite: A spiral stair leads to a lower guest room and the wine cellar.

Terry reduced the apparent size of the house by nestling it into the steep slope. The French doors of the master bedroom open to a balcony, while the guest room enjoys a secluded lower terrace.

Opposite: In the master bedroom, a mantel salvaged from a demolished Seattle mansion serves to highlight the classical nature of the columned house.

Following overleaf: A fire bowl warms the living room terrace on a chilly evening.

Terry made extensive use of salvaged materials in his home. The columns that define the plan and structure of the house were cut from enormous driftwood logs—the storm driven flotsam of the Northwest's lumber industry—that washed up on his beach. Their massy, weathered surfaces give the house the grandeur of a Greek temple, as do the rough-hewn ceiling beams that rest atop the columns, seemingly held in place by nothing more than their own great weight.[6] The roof itself is made of sod; in spring it blooms as a carpet of wildflowers. Terry's sod roof was probably inspired by the modernist Lea Fouse that Lionel Pries designed on Lopez Island in the early 1950s.[7]

In its use of primitive materials and archetypal construction, Terry's house can be seen as a twentieth-century version of the "primitive hut" of Abbé Laugier, the eithteenth-century neoclassicist who proposed that architecture had begun in nature, with rough structures fashioned by savages from trees to provide shelter "from the careless neglect of nature."[8] Two centuries later, Terry built his own primitive hut to revel in nature on his own artful terms; such was the evolution that had occurred in man's view of nature as he established his technological dominion over it.

The large living room is at the center of the house, flanked by the kitchen and dining room at the east end, and by the master bedroom and bath at the west end. The long walls of the living room are floor-to-ceiling glass doors; when they are fully retracted the living room is transformed into an open-air loggia, separated from outdoors by nothing but its columns. The floor is made of aggregate concrete; it extends to the adjoining outdoor terraces, further blurring the boundaries of interior and exterior space. The concrete is inset with whorls of tile depicting tidal currents, as if the ocean itself might wash in and out of the living room.

Throughout much of the house Terry used salvaged barn siding for interior wall sheathing, but in the living room he installed a set of boiseries that he had rescued from the demolition of a Seattle mansion. Stripped of their paint, this French paneling contributes a note of worn elegance to the room. Like the elegantly shuttered French doors that circle the exterior, the boiseries remind us of the romantic neoclassical spirit that lies below the surface of this modern house.

When Roland Terry retired from architecture in the early 1990s, he sold his property on Lopez Island. Fortunately for all concerned, the buyer was an aficionado of Terry's work who has happily dedicated himself to the preservation of this rustic modern masterpiece.

SPRUCE LODGE

SNOWMASS, COLORADO

Robert A. M. Stern Architects

1987–1991

As an author, educator, and architect, Robert A. M. Stern has been in the limelight for over two decades—first as the host of a PBS series on architecture, then on the cover of *Life* as the designer of its "American Dream House," and then later with his prolific work for the Walt Disney Company. Advertisements for luxury cooperative apartments trumpet his name as an imprimatur of quality; and when Stern added a penthouse atop his Manhattan offices—the better to focus on a workload that now includes the design of the George W. Bush Presidential Library and Museum—his new quarters were duly celebrated in *Architectural Digest*.[1]

Stern's embrace of architectural history lies at the center of his life and work. In 1998 his appointment as the Dean of Yale University's School of Architecture returned him to the cradle of his love for history. As an architecture student at Yale in the early 1960s, Stern found two mentors: Vincent Scully, the charismatic professor of architectural history, and architect Philip Johnson, who famously decreed, "You cannot not know history."[2]

Stern delights in knowing history, and integrating traditional imagery into buildings that are well-conceived and solidly made. He is unfazed by critics who dismiss his work as "retrotecture."[3] He prefers to call it "modern traditionalism."[4] Whatever it's called, Stern's approach to architecture has been pragmatic and successful; in thirty-five years his practice has grown from a little cottage industry to a well-organized hierarchy of several hundred employees.

In 1986 Stern vaulted from the ranks of New York's architectural cognoscenti to host "Pride of Place: Building the American Dream," an eight-part documentary shown on PBS. His affection for gilded-age resorts, streetcar suburbs, and early skyscrapers was contagious; his public career as an impresario of architectural history had begun.

Above: Living room chandeliers are shaped like teepees and decorated with Native American figures.

Opposite: The grand living room serves as the circulation hub of the lodge. Stairs rise—on the left—to bedrooms for guests and children, and—on the far wall—to the master suite. A freestanding chimney of Colorado sandstone anchors the room.

The commission for Spruce Lodge came at this early stage of Stern's ascendancy. Today it stands as a harbinger of his mature work. A retrospective visit reveals qualities that have shaped his buildings right down to this day: a keen awareness of site and context, a penchant for drama, a lush unity of architecture and decoration, and a knowing use of historic imagery.

The commission presented Stern with an enviable site: a ledge above a pristine valley, ringed by mountains. No other buildings are in sight, giving it even more of the air of a remote Shangri-La. Yet the resort town of Aspen sprawls just a few valleys away, offering a surfeit of glitz and bling and, more to the point, an airport. The ascent from Aspen to Spruce Lodge requires an hour's journey over increasingly rugged roads. Pavement gives way to dirt, and houses grow fewer and larger before vanishing entirely. In winter, snowbanks frame the icy road, providing a further frisson of adventure for visitors. Finally a ranch gate frames a driveway, which twists through several dips before rising to Spruce Lodge.

Trees grow thick along the drive that parallels the north face of the lodge, denying a full view of it. Roofs are pulled low over massive log walls; gables are clipped with jerkin heads. At first glance Spruce Lodge appears to be an oddly unassuming structure, because Stern—like the designers of Kildare Club and Camp Topridge—has observed the tradition of subordinating a lodge to its setting, and revealing its true splendor only gradually.

Above: A cozy inglenook within the study. This intimate room, low-ceilinged and dark, contrasts with the bright and soaring living room.

Opposite: Much of the living room's sturdy furniture was designed by Thomas Molesworth and manufactured by his Shoshone Furniture Company. Molesworth furniture—part rustic, part cowboy, part Deco—was once regarded as kitsch, but is now widely prized, collected, and imitated.

Under a porte-cochere, double entrance doors open into a low vestibule, which leads in turn to the dramatic living room. This double-height space serves as the circulation hub of the entire lodge. A remarkable stair capers around much of the room, providing a theatrical setting for entrances and exits. Balconies overlook the living room from both ends, providing visual links between the great room and the bedrooms above it.

At opposite ends, the living room opens into low-ceilinged spaces: the dining room, and an intimate study. Much of the long south wall is glass: a double-height picture window and tall doors leading to a terrace. Porches extend across the southern façade of the lodge, framing the mountain views beyond.

The western-themed decoration of the lodge is thoroughly developed and detailed. In a corner of the dining room, a sconce has been fashioned from an elk horn, with a shade made of cowhide. A curtain rod mimics a tree branch. Curtains are trimmed with grommets and leather laces inspired by horse tack; the tieback culminates in a silver spur.

Opposite: The double-height boot room serves as a vestibule to the garage, lending architectural drama to everyday comings and goings.

With its flowing spaces, dramatic stairs, and large porches, Spruce Lodge resembles nothing so much as a venerable Shingle Style house, but one built with the characteristic log construction and twig detailing of the Adirondacks. The architect's command of history appears in his ability to create such a stylistic hybrid, fill it with a fanciful Cowboys-and-Indians décor, and have it all come out feeling authentic. This is the "traditional" aspect of Stern's Modern Traditionalism.

The "modern" aspect of Modern Traditionalism can be seen in Stern's reconciliation of his clients' nostalgia for a traditional lodge with their need for a functional vacation home. The clients do not travel with a retinue of servants in the manner of Marjorie Merriweather Post, so Spruce Lodge has no servants' quarters, staff dining room, butler's pantry, or backstair—all features once found in houses of comparable size and grandeur. Family members drive their own cars, so a large garage is built right into the lodge; the adjacent boot room is an informal vestibule for everyday comings and goings. The modern kitchen is now a center for family life and entertaining, not a workroom for servants, so it is plainly visible from the living room and separated from the dining room by little more than a counter.

The bathroom of an old lodge was likely to be shoehorned under a staircase, and lit by a bare bulb. Today, the mere presence of indoor plumbing is no longer considered a luxury, and even such amenities as heated towel racks, large mirrors and flattering lighting have become standard issue. The many bathrooms of Spruce Lodge possess these modern necessities, together with carefully chosen reproduction fixtures and dignified cabinetry and tile work—in short, modern bathrooms from a traditional never-never land.

A similar approach to reconciling the modern and the traditional was taken in the design of the indoor swimming pool. With little rustic precedent for such a room—even Mrs. Post might have gaped at such an extravagance in a rustic lodge!—Stern turned to classicism for inspiration. After all, what could be more like an indoor swimming pool than a Roman bath? And weren't Greek temples originally built of wood? And certainly Stern knew of the lobby of Montana's Glacier Park Lodge, where towering tree trunks are styled as classical columns.

So the pool became a classical design executed in rustic materials, with the warm hues and rough textures of its knotty paneling and granite paving establishing a visual harmony with the rest of Spruce Lodge. And can it be a coincidence that the columns and entablatures are detailed in what classicists call the *rustic* order? No, most likely it is a knowing little joke about architectural history, courtesy of Robert A. M. Stern.

Above: Compared to the guest room (right) the master bed-room is a comfortably understated room. The door at the rear leads to an elaborate dressing room and bath; the door at left opens to the stair landing above the living room.
A landscape by Marsden Hartley hangs above a bed that recalls the late Victorian taste for faux bamboo furniture.

Right: The principal guest room envelops its occupants in an Adirondacks fantasia. Birch bark is applied to the ceiling like wallpaper, with split tree limbs to cover the seams. The balcony overlooks the living room below.

Rustic porch furniture and potted ferns are arranged around the pool, as in a Victorian hothouse. A painted backdrop depicting Sergeant Preston—a fictional Canadian Mountie in a 1950s television series—adds a campy note of make-believe rusticity.

Right: The indoor swimming pool combines classical architecture with rustic materials. Above the water, a flock of stylized geese flies south.

Overleaf: Early morning on the porch of the master bedroom.

160

RUSTIC REDUX

NEW YORK STATE

Shope Reno Wharton and Assocciates

2000–2002

Root burls were fashioned into stair balusters.

Tʜᴇ ᴀʀᴄʜɪᴛᴇᴄᴛꜱ ᴏꜰ Sʜᴏᴘᴇ Rᴇɴᴏ Wʜᴀʀᴛᴏɴ are known for designing expansive homes for well-heeled clients. Much of the firm's work has been done along the coasts of Connecticut and Long Island, where the Shingle Style flourished a century ago. In these settings the architects perfected a style of house—replete with stately columns, shady porches, majestic fireplaces, inviting window seats, lush gardens, and lovely swimming pools—that conjures a perfected world of old money and Waspy good taste.

The rolling New York farmland surrounding this family vacation home offered little in the way of architectural inspiration for a rustic dwelling. But inspiration was found nearby; in a cabin that Allan Shope—a founding partner of Shope Reno Wharton—had built for his family. The cabin measures only nine hundred square feet, but it is a masterpiece of rustic craftsmanship. Like the Adirondack craftsmen who built Camp Pine Knot, Shope gathered his materials from the surrounding woods: pine trees were milled into floor boards, cedar branches were fashioned into stair rails, and granite slabs framed the fireplace.[1]

This creative recycling appealed to the architects' new client, who set about culling dead trees from his estate. Cedars were kept whole for use as columns; cherry, pine, and walnut trees were milled on the property for siding and planking.

The house was built on high ground, with magnificent views of distant hills and valleys. To downplay its size, the architects divided the formal and informal areas of the house into two wings. The informal areas—the children's playroom, dressing rooms for the pool, laundry, and garage—were placed in the smaller north wing. The apparent size of the formal south wing was further reduced by the shadowy recesses of its encompassing porches, and by gabled roofs that subsume the second floor within their downward sweeping planes.

Elaborately carved birds roost on the newel posts of the double stair.

The foursquare architecture of this house serves as a calm and ordered backdrop for its intensely developed detailing. The exuberance of the interior is foretold at the gabled entrance, where four cedar trees are woven into a screen wall framing the front door. The Adirondack architect William Coulter attached similar screen walls—meticulously assembled from sections of logs—to the gabled porches of the Knollwood Club on Saranac Lake in 1899; the screen wall devised by Shope Reno Wharton is a wild and woolly reinterpretation of such a porch.

The front door opens directly into the two-story living room. This vast space is decked out with rustic masterials imported directly from the out-of-doors. The result is a fanastic forest, like the lobby of Old Faithful Inn on a diet of Miracle-Gro. From just inside the front door, twin stairs sweep up to a bridge that spans the living room, then leads to twin galleries overlooking twin fireplaces, before continuing on to bedrooms beyond. The

The living room is an elegant forest of exuberant rustic craftsmanship.

The restrained decoration of the dining room provides a background for New Trails, *a painting by N.C. Wyeth.*

enormous walk-in fireplaces are faced in beautiful courses of fragmented local stone; the fire screens are fancifully decorated with metal silhouettes of woodland flora and fauna.

The upper levels of the living room are supported on cedar trees used as columns, with their branches stretching to the vaulted ceiling. Railings were fashioned from branches cut from a drought-stricken thicket of mountain laurel. Where disease had created root burls, these branches were used as stair balusters, with the burls suggesting traditional ball-and-claw feet.

Floorboards were cut from the full width of the trunks of cherry trees, with their edges retaining the natural shape of the tree. The boards were then carefully fit together, so that the floors echo the irregular outlines of a grove of trees. Each board was then scraped to produce a slight crown along its length. The result: floors that appear to ripple, like the surface of a lake touched by a light breeze. The simple act of crossing the room becomes a walking meditation, an experience that suggests that the architects of Shope Reno Wharton have discovered a new form of contemplation in the rustic tradition.

Opposite: Porch posts were cut from gnarled cedar trees, with many branches left intact.

A MODERN
LOG CABIN

JACKSON, WYOMING

Cesar Pelli & Associates

1990–1993

The wetlands around this vacation home include a pond populated by swans and ducks.

I<small>N A CAREER</small> spanning half a century, Cesar Pelli has designed airports, museums, libraries, theaters, a score of skyscrapers and a handful of private homes. Pelli does not have a signature style, a characteristic that can be traced to his apprenticeship with Eero Saarinen, who rejected the one-style-fits-all doctrine of Miesian modernism. In Saarinen's office, Pelli worked on projects as diverse as the bird-like TWA terminal at Kennedy airport and the medieval-modern complex of Morse and Stiles Colleges at Yale University.

In his own practice, Pelli has tempered Saarinen's eclecticism with an abiding interest in context and history: the Winter Garden of the World Financial Center attests to his fascination with Joseph Paxton's Crystal Palace; the courtyards and tower of a classroom complex on the Riverside campus of the University of California pay homage to that city's famed Mission Inn; the richly patterned facades of Carnegie Hall Tower in New York complement the Victorian ornament of the adjacent concert hall without descending into imitation.[1]

In designing a vacation home in Jackson Hole, Pelli faced a contextual issue that often arises in the West: what does one build in a place of great natural beauty, where the only authentic local building type is the humble log cabin? The growth of Jackson Hole from a remote ranching valley to a tourist mecca occurred in less than a century, far too short a time for a local architectural tradition to evolve. In place of such a tradition, an atmosphere of rustic kitsch has prevailed, fueled by Hollywood's use of the valley as a location for such westerns as *The Big Sky*, *The Big Trail*, and *Shane*. The architectural manifestations of this atmosphere range from the high camp of a Maverik gas station lodged in a tiny replica of the Old Faithful Inn, to the too-tasteful design guidelines promulgated by developers of half-acre lots carved out of old cattle ranches.

Opposite: A pathway banked with wildflowers leads to the front door.

174

Behind a screen of columns, stairs rise to a mezzanine.

Opposite: The living room is the social center and circulation hub of the house

The house that Pelli designed is set amidst lush wetlands on the floodplains of the Snake River, a landscape of great primordial beauty. Spring-fed streams meander through grasslands turned bright green by the abundance of water. Willows and towering old cottonwoods shade an idyllic pond, home to a nesting pair of swans. The treetops part to reveal glimpses of the craggy peaks of the Teton Mountains.

The owners of this property began their quest for a family vacation home modestly enough: they looked at plans for pre-designed log homes. Having worked with Pelli in several philanthropic endeavors, the couple sought his advice in selecting among a number of such designs.

Pelli, at once tactful and persuasive, suggested that such a magnificent property called for a commensurately magnificent building, and that he would be happy to design such a building for the couple. The distance that was ultimately traveled in this aesthetic journey is now memorialized by the inscription embroidered on a sofa pillow in the soaring living room of the house that Pelli designed: "Welcome To Our Log Cabin."

Two sets of double doors connect the intimate dining room to the living room.

Bead board walls are hung with photographs by Edward S. Curtis.

Eschewing rustic kitsch, Pelli designed a house scaled to the grandeur of the setting, a house that draws inspiration from the ancient roots of architecture in the natural world. The elongated dimensions of the house, approximately 140 feet long and 50 feet wide, reflect its immediate site, a narrow peninsula that rises imperceptibly from surrounding wetlands. In this fertile landscape, the house resembles a grove of trees grown tall along a stream bank, a metaphor made real by the fifty-five columns—some as tall as thirty feet—that were cut from a stand of dead Engelmann spruce.

The tallest trees form a two-story colonnade soaring up to a rooftop clerestory; the colonnade runs through the house like a spine, uniting horizontal and vertical circulation. The more public areas of the house—living room, dining room and kitchen on the lower floor, a library on the upper floor—are grouped along the west side of the colonnade, facing the Tetons through walls of windows. Bedrooms and other private quarters are entered from the east side of the colonnade.

At the southern end of the house, the colonnade ends in a mudroom entrance connected to a garage; to the north it bursts free from the walls of the house, like a towering porch marching into the untamed landscape. Here the gabled colonnade assumes its most classical appearance, reminding us of Abbé Laugier's primitive hut, and of ancient Greek temples—like the Temple of Hera at Olympia—which were built of wood before they were rebuilt in stone.

The rough cedar cladding of the house is accented at regular intervals by slender boards of smoothly milled cedar. These accents coincide with the wood window frames, thus wrapping the entire house in a subtle horizontal banding. This patterning is carried into the house by the dimensions of the post-and-beam framing.

In the living room the horizontal module establishes the rectilinear patterns of shelving and paneling; in the dining room it appears in the divisions of the bead board walls. This grid-like patterning of the house can be seen as another allusion to classical architecture; here, to the neoclassicism of Jean-Nicolas-Louis Durand, who sought to reduce design to the manipulation of a system of grids and modules.[2]

While Pelli may allude to such theoretical dogma in his design, he does not subjugate the design to the dogma. Rather than designing the building to suit the grid, he has designed the grid to suit the building. The asymmetrical massing and irregular outline of the house were shaped by the varying dimensions of the spaces within. Even the central colonnade was subject to adjustment: where it opens to the entrance hall and the living room, the interval between the columns is increased to make for an easy flow of space.

The living room exemplifies Pelli's ability to synthesize classical order and informal, picturesque planning. The rectilinear proportions of the room are animated by the upward sweep of the stair and the downward plunge of the roof. The elegant grids of the stair and mezzanine are played against the brute strength of the columns that surround them, and the exquisitely proportioned window walls frame the ever-shifting spectacles of nature just outside.

Opposite: The north porch serves as a walkway into nature.

Preceding Overleaf: Mortise-and-tenon joints connect beams of Douglas fir to columns of Engelmann spruce; metal straps secure the connections.

Following Overleaf: A rustic bench overlooks the Snake River and the Teton Mountains.

LEDGE HOUSE

CATOCTIN MOUNTAINS, MARYLAND

Bohlin Cywinski Jackson

1992–1996

A portal of logs, resembling the torii gate of a Shinto shrine, frames the entrance to Ledge House.

Right: The vestibule occupies a break in the formidable log wall that surrounds the entry court.

Iₙ THE DAYS BEFORE AIR-CONDITIONING, many of Washington's leading citizens fled the summer heat that blankets the low-lying capital city—a tradition that lives on today in the Congressional summer recess. Others took to higher ground. Abraham Lincoln and his family spent more than a quarter of his presidency in a spacious Gothic Revival cottage on the grounds of Soldiers' Home, three and a half miles from the White House, and 200 feet higher.

In the 1870s the Western Maryland Railroad opened the Catoctin Mountains to tourism. Resorts with hotels, cottages and amusement parks were developed at Pen Mar (elevation 1300 feet) and Braddock Heights (elevation 950 feet). Summer visitors from Washington and Baltimore brought a measure of prosperity to a hardscrabble Appalachian economy based on subsistence farming and the logging, mining, and quarrying operations involved in producing iron at the Catoctin Furnace. The furnace, a relic of colonial industry, was gradually rendered obsolete and unprofitable by the growth of the steel industry in the late nineteenth century. It was blown out in 1903 and soon fell into ruin.

In 1929 Lawrence Richey, private secretary and loyal factotum to President Herbert Hoover, bought 1800 acres of forested land just west of Catoctin Furnace. He built a fishing camp that became a favored country retreat for the President and other members of Washington's ruling elite.

A severe drought gripped the Catoctin Mountains in the early 1930s; followed by forest fires that compounded the damage done by decades of clear-cutting for farming, bark stripping for tanning, and logging for charcoal making. *The Baltimore Sun* surveyed the damage in 1935: "Today whole groves of gray, ghostly trunks, stripped of bark and leaves, testify to the completeness of the destruction."[1]

*The ledge circles the living room, with its irregular
steps forming a natural amphitheatre.*

The exposed framing of the kitchen recalls the primitive construction of simple summer cottages. A further note of informality is introduced by the use of exposed electrical conduit and industrial receptacles.

Opposite: The post-and-beam framing system sails through the kitchen window, suggesting that the boundaries of indoors and out are quite flexible at Ledge House.

Efforts to restore the Catoctin forest began during the New Deal, when the federal government launched initiatives to extend the benefits of the back-to-nature movement to the urban working class. A study conducted by the National Park Service summarized the ideals that motivated these initiatives:

> Man's loss of intimate contact with nature has had debilitating effects on him as a being which can be alleviated only by making it possible for him to escape at frequent intervals from his urban habitat to the open country…He must again learn how to enjoy himself in the out-of-doors by reacquiring the environmental knowledge and skills he has lost during his exile from his natural environment.[2]

The Catoctin Mountains were designated a Recreational Demonstration Area because of their proximity to the urban populations of both Washington and Baltimore. The federal government bought up 10,000 acres of exhausted farmland and degraded forests and redeveloped them for public recreation. Workers demolished old farms, leveled stone fences, tore up miles of meandering roads, dammed streams to make swimming holes, and planted thousands of trees and shrubs. Lumber milled from blighted trees was used to build three cabin complexes— Camp Misty Mount, Camp Greentop and Camp Hi-Catoctin.

In 1942, President Franklin Roosevelt's doctors suggested that mountain air might provide relief for his respiratory ailments and chronic sinusitis. The ensuing search for a high-elevation retreat near Washington led to Camp Hi-Catoctin. Delighted with the camp's beauty and air of isolation, Roosevelt named it "Shangri-La" after the fictional Himalayan utopia of *Lost Horizon*; President Dwight Eisenhower renamed it after his grandson: Camp David.

Today, the land acquired during the New Deal is shared by Cunningham Falls State Park and Catoctin Mountain Park, which surrounds Camp David. Restoration and regeneration have given rise to a second-growth forest of maple, hickory, cherry, and oak, and a habitat for wildlife—wild turkeys, mink, beavers, and black bears—that had vanished from the region.

In the early 1990s a family from Washington began planning a weekend house on land adjoining this restored forest, near the streams where Herbert Hoover once stalked trout in his waist-high waders and suit and tie. The family had vacationed at The Point (pages 92-103) and they imagined a similar setting of casual rustic elegance, sturdily built of logs, stone and heavy timbers. After poring over a copy of Harvey Kaiser's *Great Camps of the Adirondacks*, they called its author about their plans, and Kaiser referred them to an old friend, architect Peter Bohlin.

The screened porch offers a shady setting for summer dining.

Bohlin, a founding partner of Bohlin Cywinski Jackson, had recently designed a lodge on Lake George that was much admired for its adaptation of traditional Adirondack architecture to the program of a modern vacation home. He was also designing a summer home on Lake Michigan, in which the familiar form of a woodland cottage contained streamlined rooms paneled in Douglas fir, with a central fireplace core made of concrete slabs in place of stone.

When the family from Washington asked Bohlin to design their weekend home in the Catoctins, he recognized that the project invited a more abstract approach to rustic imagery than he had employed in these earlier projects. The mountains of Maryland lack a well-defined local building tradition like those of the Adirondacks and the upper Michigan peninsula; and the family's requirements included such features as an indoor swimming pool that might well appear incongruous in a traditionally rustic setting.

Opposite: White cedar logs rise from the hillside to support the porch. Shrouds of hammered lead protect logs that are exposed to the weather.

Instead of designing a house with a literal resemblance to an Adirondack lodge, Bohlin set about designing an abstraction of such a lodge; in his words "a stirring place that fit our clients' wishes and revealed the particular nature of its time, place, and making."[3] These efforts led to his re-imagining the essential attributes of a rustic retreat—a vast fireplace and screened porch, massive stones and mighty logs, sheltering roofs and expansive windows—in a structure rooted in the Catoctin forest.

The place chosen by Bohlin and his clients was a plateau on a wooded hillside, once the site of a cabin built during the 1940s. A ledge of eroded stone defined the southern edge of the plateau; beyond it a sunny deciduous forest descended to a cascading stream. To Bohlin, the crumbling edges of the plateau suggested "the remains of a quarry one might come upon in the forest."[4] The evocative quality of that ledge would inspire both the design of the house and its name: Ledge House.

The existing ledge was given greater heft—both literally and symbolically—by the addition of layer upon layer of stone, some sixty truckloads in all, imported from Lake Champlain. Bohlin selected this quartzite stone because it resembled the native stone of the ledge, while possessing a superior strength that allowed it to be quarried in monumental slabs.

This effort to accentuate the suggestive quality of the ledge harkens back to the picturesque belief that man is capable of improving nature, by sensing the spirit of a place and concentrating it through design. This belief inspired the National Park Service guidelines that led to the restoration of the Catoctin forest as a pristine wilderness, in which the streams are well stocked with trout for the convenience of fly-casting sportsmen. It also inspired Olmsted's designs for the landscape that surrounds the Ames Gate Lodge, where enormous fieldstones were buried to reinforce the romantic impression of a rugged glacial moraine.

In Bohlin's design, the ledge serves as the foundation for a wall of stacked logs that defines the entry court. The wall delays a visitor's discovery of the valley below the house, while giving the north side of the house an impressively fortified appearance. Gaps between the ends of logs create tiny windows like the embrasures of a colonial fort; several are placed mischievously close to the ground, as if for the benefit of the family dog.

The log walls part at the center of the courtyard, where a portal of logs, resembling the torii gate of a Shinto shrine, marks the entrance to the house. Behind this portal, a projecting glass vestibule rises to the roof of the house in a grandly welcoming gesture. Beneath an abstract metal frieze of evergreen trees, a weighty door built of wood planks adds another note of grandeur to the entrance.

The exposed framing of the master bedroom is partially covered in carefully detailed panels of plywood.

Opposite: The master suite is sumptuously appointed with built-in storage. The bed was designed as an integral part of the cabinetry.

The stone ledge continues under the log walls, bringing the landscape into the house. It runs from the forecourt through the vestibule, and then drops three steps to the wood floor of the grandly scaled living room. The ledge extends in an arc from the log wall on the north side of the room to the massive fireplace and chimney wall on the west. As it traces this irregular curve, the stepped edges of the ledge form an amphitheater facing into the room. With the addition of pillows, this Paleolithic built-in furniture becomes a comfortable gathering place.

The living room overlooks the forest through an expanse of glass reaching from wall-to-wall and floor-to-ceiling. Attenuated mullions frame the individual windows, forming a delicate rectilinear tracery of wood. The green canopy of the forest extends right up to the glass, shading it from the high arc of the summer sun. In winter, the sun reaches deep into the room, casting shadows from the bare treetops as it skims the hills to the south.

The tilted roof of the living room is supported by a dazzling system of angular post-and-beam framing. Douglas fir posts on the north side of the room rise at a right angle to the roof, causing them to lean into the space; the posts on the south side of the room are rise at right angles to the floor. The columns are joined to the ceiling beams by galvanized steel brackets with large springs that tighten the joints as the beams shrink. The result is a structural dance akimbo, accented by percussive glints of silver. The multiplication of structural members and the expressive detailing of their connections recall the craftsmanship of the winter home that Greene & Greene designed for Charles Millard Pratt (pages 82-91), where much of the beauty of the house is derived from the articulation of its structure, down to the binding of its corbelled beams with sinuous iron straps.

At Ledge House, the structural framing of the living room is redeployed in the even larger space that houses the swimming pool. The ledge takes on a particularly rugged appearance here. From within the pool it resembles the shattered rock face of a flooded quarry. Across the room, large doors open to a terrace and a view of the valley below. The tilted roof floats above a continuous surround of windows that admit light from all sides. Reflections of the surrounding forest dance across the water.

The architectural wit that underlies the exuberant detailing of Ledge House becomes explicit in what Peter Bohlin refers to as the "mouse-bite" door: a rolling door of galvanized steel that secures the entrance to the pool. The leading edge of the door is cut to match the irregular profile of the logs and stone of the wall that it closes against. As the door rolls shut, it nestles snugly into place. A pane of glass is set within the door, neither too high nor too low, but just right for a child to gaze at the pool in wonder.

Opposite: When the "mouse-bite" door is closed, it fits snugly against the wall to the left.

The swimming pool was designed to blur the boundaries of inside and out, natural and man-made.

Following overleaf: At the west end of Ledge House, the master bedroom projects into the trees, and the log walls of the house reach into the landscape. Long boards hovering from the eaves extend the rooflines, like the chigi finials of traditional Japanese roofs.

LONG RESIDENCE

ORCAS ISLAND, WASHINGTON

Cutler Anderson

2003

Not long after he opened his architectural practice on Bainbridge Island in 1977, James Cutler was designing a home on the island, for a setting he recalls as "an ethereal forest, a fantastic place."[1] After Cutler opposed clear-cutting the site to facilitate construction, the client summoned him to a meeting on the property, which had just been reduced to a landscape of smoldering stumps. Cutler recalls his reaction:

> I turned to the owner and said, "You've just made me realize that I'm part of a rapacious system that's devouring the planet and no matter how good a job I do, I just make it worse." And—this is pretty close to a direct quote—the owner said, "Jim, I'm not into anything as cosmic as that. I just want to impress my friends and be able to see the house from a distance."[2]

In the aftermath of this debacle, Cutler inverted the usual relationship of client and architect, and took to interviewing his potential clients to see if they were sufficiently committed to his belief that buildings must honor the land they occupy.

This retreat home on Orcas Island exemplifies Cutler's talent for shaping his environmental ideals into buildings that are beautiful and emotionally satisfying for their occupants. The setting is a forested slope on the island's southern shore, overlooking a saltwater channel traversed by the green and white ferries that link the San Juan Islands to the mainland.

A concrete plinth is sunk into the slope, retaining earth to the north and rising as a broad terrace to the south. Set atop the plinth is a modern version of that most primitive of woodland structures: a lean-to shelter. The tilt of the shed roof opens the house to sunlight and water views to the south, while concealing it from the easement road that marks the northern edge of the property. From the road, the roof almost disappears beneath a carpet of fallen pine needles, completing the disguise of the house within its natural setting.

Living and dining areas occupy a great room punctuated by log tripods that hold the roof aloft.

Following overleaf: The kitchen is an island of fine carpentry floating at the far end of the great room.

*The curtainless bedroom might please Thoreau: "I have an appointment with spring.
She comes to the window to wake me, and I go forth an hour or two earlier than usual."*

A terrace overlooking the water runs the length of the house. Its sleek detailing recalls Le Corbusier's fascination with the modernity of ocean liners.

The interior is dominated by a one-of-a-kind structural system that supports the roof. Eighteen tripods lift six giant logs into the air; the logs serve as beams carrying the rafters. The tripods are joined to the beams by hidden steel plates; they also drop through the floor to footings in the basement.

The cedar trees used for the beams and tripods were cut from land owned by the contractor's father, then carefully stripped of their bark to emphasize their sculptural qualities. While these organic forms, inspired by the installations of fallen trees created by Scottish sculptor Andy Goldsworthy,[3] were intended to evoke the surrounding forest, they may also remind us of the efforts that early hunter and trappers made to improvise temporary structures from woodland materials, as they sought shelter in the uncharted wilderness.

The structural framework of the house is wrapped in curtain walls of glass. The ends of the house are partially filled with shingled panels for privacy's sake, but the south wall rises fifteen feet in a continuous expanse of glazing. Refined carpentry and a subdued color palette make the interior of the house a quiet backdrop for the drama of the symbolic trees rising within it, and the forest towering without.

Disembodied by its glass enclosure, this modern lean-to merges with its forest setting.

RIDGE HOUSE

SPOKANE, WASHINGTON

Olson Sundberg Kundig Allen

2001

The towering front door is decorated with a metal bas-relief of organic forms created by Harold Balazs, a local artist and a frequent collaborator in architectural projects. Kundig once worked as an apprentice in Balazs' studio, and credits the artist with inspiring him "to think of the architectural enterprise as expansive and inclusive instead of the introspective and contemplative endeavors encountered in school."[1]

Opposite: Ridge House shares the dynamic angularity and elegant proportions that characterize much of Kundig's work. The use of wood siding and stone relate the house to its rugged setting, and to the traditions of rustic architecture.

T OM KUNDIG, a partner in the Seattle firm of Olson Sundberg Kundig Allen, has received many awards and accolades for a series of houses that relate to the landscape in unusual ways. Chicken Point Cabin (2002) is a concrete box with a six-ton window wall that opens on horizontal pivots to a view of Idaho's Hayden Lake. Delta Shelter (2005) is a three-story cabin raised on stilts above a flood plain in Washington's Methow Valley. A hand crank opens and closes steel shutters that protect floor-to-ceiling windows on all sides of the cabin. On the same property, the Rolling Huts (2007) accommodate guests in angular, modernist cabins that are raised above a meadow on wheeled legs of steel, like primitive landing gear.

The angular forms, elegant proportions, and dramatic windows of these compact vacation retreats also appear in Ridge House, a residence that Kundig designed in 2001 for the fourth and fifth generations of a prominent Spokane family with a history of commissioning noteworthy houses. In 1903 the founder of this dynasty commissioned a residence from Kirtland Cutter, then Spokane's leading architect; the result was a Craftsman-style shingled dwelling with a dramatically plunging roofline. In 1913 a commission from the same tycoon for a winter home in Santa Barbara led to the beginning of Cutter's prolific late career in southern California.[2]

Kundig's design for Ridge House is at once innovative and traditional; a duality that is reflected in his larger career. He is both a designer of striking originality, and the latest prominent figure in an architectural tradition of the Pacific Northwest that emphasizes the integration of well-made buildings and natural landscapes. This lineage of formidable talents includes Kirtland Cutter, Ellsworth Storey, Wade Hampton Pipes, A. E. Doyle, Pietro Belluschi, John Yeon, Lionel Pries, Paul Hayden Kirk, and Roland Terry.

The living room floats above the surrounding landscape. Architectural detailing is kept to a minimum,
and the traditional elements of many rustic interiors—
moose heads, bearskin rugs, and twiggy furniture—have
been banished, in deference to the room's sweeping
views of the natural world.

216

As its name suggests, Ridge House is situated on high ground, in a semi-arid pine forest on the outskirts of Spokane. The owners of the property could hardly have chosen an architect with a better understanding of their land: Tom Kundig grew up nearby, and he recalls his joy in roaming this forest as a teenager.

The undulating crest of the ridge inspired him to design Ridge House as a series of wooden boxes bridging the depressions that time had carved into the land. At the north end of the house, a double-height living room spans the deepest gap like a glassy Ponte Vecchio; at the south end an open-air catwalk connects the master bedroom to a home office in a small structure, dubbed "the fort," that stands apart from the rest of the house as a place of work and privacy.

The living room contains discrete areas for living and dining; the low-ceilinged kitchen is adjacent to the dining area. The long walls of this grand room are made entirely of windows, with views of a horse pasture to the west and the deep forest to the east. Badgers and deer are often scene walking beneath the house; the windows also allow the family's two golden retrievers to track the movements of a roving barn cat.

At the end of the room, the traditional rustic elements of a stone fireplace and chimney are reduced to their essential forms. The chimney rises outside the room, separated from the rectangular chimneybreast by a wall of glass. Flanking the fireplace are venerable family andirons that depict dragons in wrought iron; the mantel above is a simple shelf of thick steel. The traditional inglenook is moved over to one side, where it juts out beyond the rest of the room to provide yet another perspective of the forest; its built-in cabinetry contains toys, board games, and the inevitable television set.

While such a room—a large space focused on a hearth, but with expansive windows in opposite walls—is rarely found in conventional houses of any size, we have seen it in a variety of rustic dwellings, from the recreation room of the Kildare Club and the bedrooms of Camp Wonundra, to the living rooms of the Charles Millard Pratt House, Camp Topridge, Fortune Rock, and Roland Terry's weekend house. Kundig has described the deep appeal of such rooms by referring to the theory of "prospect and refuge" proposed by the English geographer Jay Appleton: "It goes back to when people lived in high cave shelters overlooking a horizon. The dark secure area of the cave is the refuge. The horizon below is where the critters are. People can leave the refuge to explore, and return to it for safety."[3]

At Ridge House, Tom Kundig has reimagined the rustic home as an elegant refuge from the uncertain prospects of life in the twenty-first century.

A soaring glass enclosure opens the master bedroom to views of the forest floor below and the stars above.

Following overleaf: A stream winds through the valley below Ridge House.

BIBLIOGRAPHY

Albrecht, Donald, Robert Schonfeld, and Lindsay Stamm Shapiro. *Russel Wright: Creating American Lifestyle*. New York: Smithsonian Institution/ Abrams, 2001.

Amory, Cleveland. *The Last Resorts*. New York: Harper & Brothers, 1948.

Bosley, Edward R. *Greene & Greene*. London: Phaidon Press, 2000.

Branch, Mark Alden. "Blast from the Past." *Yale Alumni Magazine* vol. 62 (March 1999): 24-31.

Brown, Patricia Leigh. "Out-Twigging the Neighbors: In the Adirondacks, Great Camps Are Sprouting Again." *The New York Times*, 23 October 1997: F1.

"Charms of the Adirondacks." *The New York Times*, 22 July 1894: 9.

Davis, A. J. *Rural Residences*. New York: Alexander Jackson Davis, 1837.

Donaldson, Alfred Lee. *A History of the Adirondacks*. New York: The Century Co., 1921.

Downing, A. J. *The Architecture of Country Houses*. New York: D. Appleton & Co., 1859.

—————. *A Treatise on the Theory and Practice of Landscape Gardening, Adapted to North America; With a View to the Improvement of Country Residences*. New York: Orange Judd Agricultural Book Publisher, 1865.

Drucker, Stephen. "Arts and Crafts Cabin: An Architect's One-Room Retreat in New York." *Architectural Digest* vol. 53 no. 6 (June 1996): 158-161, 202.

Evans, Tony. "A Moving Experience: Tom Kundig designs Sun Valley Center for the Arts' new facility." *Idaho Arts Quarterly* vol. 1 no.26 (2 September-1 December 2008): 18.

Faber, Harold. "State Sells Its Lavish Camp in Adirondacks for $911,000." *The New York Times*, 1 August 1985: B2.

Floyd, Margaret Henderson. *Henry Hobson Richardson: A Genius for Architecture*. New York: Monacelli Press, 1997.

Ford, Ford Madox. *The Great Trade Route*. New York: Oxford University Press, 1937.

Fox, Pamela W. *North Shore Boston: Country Houses Of Essex County, 1865-1930*. New York: Acanthus Press, 2005.

Friedman, Daniel J. "The Kildare Club." *ALA News* (2006): 6-8.

Gilborn, Craig. *Adirondack Camps: Homes Away from Home, 1850-1950*. Syracuse: Adirondack Museum/ Syracuse University Press, 2000.

Gilman, Benjamin Ives. "Charles Greely Loring." In *Museum of Fine*

Arts, Boston: Twenty-Seventh Annual Report for the Year 1902, 3-10. Cambridge: The University Press, 1903.

Giovannini, Joseph. "Miracle on 34th Street: Robert A. M. Stern Dramatically Reinvents a Rooftop Shed for Himself in Manhattan." *Architectural Digest* vol. 64 no. 7 (July 2007): 32-41.

Girouard, Mark. "The House and the Natural Landscape: A Prelude to Fallingwater." In *Fallingwater, a Frank Lloyd Wright Country House*, Edgar Kaufmann, Jr., 14-23. New York: Abbeville Press, 1986.

Goldberger, Paul. "Skyscrapers Battle It Out Near Carnegie Hall." *The New York Times*, 21 October 1990: section 2, 38.

Haynes, Wesley. "The Adirondack Camp In American Architecture." *Adirondack Camps Theme Study*: www.nps.gov/nhl/themes/Architecture/2camp.pdf, 2000.

Hearn, Millard F. *Ideas That Shape Buildings*. Cambridge: MIT Press, 2003.

Henderson, Justin. *Roland Terry: Master Northwest Architect*. Seattle: University of Washington Press, 2000.

Hijiya, James A. "Four Ways of Looking at a Philanthropist." *Proceedings of the American Philosophical Society* vol. 124 no. 6 (17 December 1980): 404-18.

Hooker, Mildred Phelps Stokes. *Camp Chronicles*. Blue Mountain Lake, NY: Adirondack Museum, 1964.

Howe, George. "Some Experiences and Observations of an Elderly Architect." *Perspecta 2, The Yale Architectural Journal*. New Haven (1953): 2-5.

Kaiser, Harvey H. *Great Camps of the Adirondacks*. Boston: David R. Godine, 1982.

Kowsky, Francis R. "H. H. Richardson's Ames Gate Lodge and the Romantic Landscape Tradition," *The Journal of the Society of Architectural Historians* vol. 50 no. 2 (June 1991): 181-188.

Kunstler, James Howard. "For Sale." *The New York Times*, 18 June 1989: section 6, 22.

Laugier, Marc-Antoine. *An Essay on Architecture* (trans. Wolfgang and Anni Herrmann). Los Angeles: Hennessy and Ingalls, 1977.

MacKay, Robert B., Anthony K. Baker, and Carol A. Traynor, eds. *Long Island Country Houses and Their Architects, 1860-1940*. New York: Society for the Preservation of Long Island Antiquities/W. W. Norton, 1997.

Macy, Christine, and Sarah Bonnemaison. *Architecture and Nature: Creating the American Landscape*. New York: Routledge, 2003.

Magoc, Chris. *Yellowstone: the Creation and Selling of an American Landscape, 1870-1903*. Albuquerque: University of New Mexico Press, 1999.

Makinson, Randell L. *Greene & Greene, Architecture as a Fine Art*. Salt Lake City: Peregrine Smith, 1977.

Manchester, Lee. "Two Camps on Osgood Pond." *Lake Placid News*, 21 & 28 July 2006:www.adirondackconnections.com/Yoga/060721%20VLP%20Osgood%20tour%20(1).pdf www.adirondackconnections.com/Yoga/060721%20VLP%20Osgood%20tour%20(2).pdf

Matthews, Henry. *Kirtland Cutter: architect in the land of promise*. Seattle: University of Washington Press, 1998.

Medgyesi, Victoria. "Long Residence." *Architectural Record* vol. 194 no. 01 (January 2006): 160-163.

"Mrs. Marjorie Merriweather Post Is Dead at 86." *The New York Times*, 13 September 1973: 50.

"Mrs. Post's Magnificent World." *Life* vol. 59 no. 19 (5 November 1965): 44-71.

Ngo, Dung, ed., *Tom Kundig: Houses*. New York: Princeton Architectural Press, 2006.

Noonan, Wendy. "Antiques: A Pioneer and a Rebel, Still a Secret." *The New York Times*, 23 May 2003: E37.

Ochsner, Jeffrey Karl, ed. *Shaping Seattle Architecture: A Historical Guide to the Architects*. Seattle: University of Washington Press, 1994.

Olsen, Richard. *Log Houses of the World*. New York: Abrams, 2006.

Pierson, Jr., William H. "The Beauty of a Belief: The Ames Family, Richardson, and Unitarianism." In *H.H. Richardson : the Architect, His Peers, and Their Era*, edited by Maureen Meister, xix-xliv. Cambridge: MIT Press, 1999.

Pulos, Arthur J. *The American Design Adventure: 1940-1975*. Cambridge: M.I.T. Press, 1988.

Quinn, Ruth. *Weaver of Dreams: The Life and Architecture of Robert C. Reamer*. Gardiner, MT: Leslie & Ruth Quinn, Publishers, 2004.

Riera Ojeda, Oscar, ed. *Ledge House*. Gloucester, MA: Rockport Publishers, 1999.

Rueda, Luis F., ed. *Robert A. M. Stern: Buildings and Projects 1981-1985*. New York: Rizzoli, 1986.

Rubin, Nancy. *American Empress: The Life and Times of Marjorie Merriweather Post*. New York: Villard Books, 1995.

Schauffler, Robert Haven. "Unique Mount Desert." *The Century Magazine* (August 1911): 477-90.

Schneider, Paul. *The Adirondacks: a History of America's First Wilderness*. New York: Henry Holt & Company, 1997.

Schulze, Franz. *Philip Johnson: Life and Work*. Chicago: University of Chicago Press, 1994.

Scully Jr., Vincent J. *The Shingle Style and The Stick Style: Architectural Theory and Design from Downing to the Origins of Wright*. New Haven: Yale University Press, 1971.

Stoddard, Seneca Ray. *The Adirondacks*. Glen Falls, NY: Seneca Ray Stoddard, 1881.

Story, Walter Rendell. "Decorative Art: Exhibit at Fair." *The New York Times*, 19 May 1940: 51

"The Railways and the California Exhibition." *Railway Age Gazette* vol. 59 no. 12 (17 September 1915): 499-502.

Thomas, Joseph B. "A Personal Remembrance of Fortune Rock." *GA Houses*, 1982, 11: 14-25.

Thoreau, Henry David; Cramer, Jeffrey S. Cramer, ed. *Walden: a fully annotated edition*. New Haven, Yale University Press, 2004.

Toker, Franklin. *Fallingwater Rising: Frank Lloyd Wright, E. J. Kaufman and America's Most Extraordinary House*. New York: Alfred A. Knopf, 2003.

U.S. Department of the Interior, National Park Service, *A Study of the Park and Recreation Problem of the United States*. Washington, D.C.: Government Printing Office, 1941.

"Unloading the Ark." *Time* vol. 85 (5 February 1965): http://www.time.com/time/magazine/article/0,9171,839254,00.html

Wehrle, Edmund F. *Catoctin Mountain Park: A Historic Resource Survey*. National Park Service, March 2000: http://www.nps.gov/archive/cato/hrs/hrs5a.htm

White, Norval, and Elliot Willensky. *AIA Guide to New York City*. New York: Crown Publishers, 2000.

Williams, Priscilla de Forest. *The Story of Wawapek, 1898-1998*. Cold Spring Harbor, NY: private printing, 1998.

Wright, Russel. *Russel Wright: Good Design is for Everyone*. New York: Universe, 2001.

Yost, L. Morgan. "Greene & Greene of Pasadena." *The Journal of the Society of Architectural Historians* vol. 9 no. 1/2 (March-May 1950): 11-19.

Zaitzevsky, Cynthia. *The Architecture of William Ralph Emerson: 1833-1917*. Cambridge: Fogg Museum, Harvard University, 1969.

NOTES

Introduction

1. Henry David Thoreau; Jeffrey S. Cramer, ed., *Walden: a fully annotated edition* (New Haven, Yale University Press, 2004), 90.

2. A. J. Downing, *A Treatise on the Theory and Practice of Landscape Gardening, Adapted to North America; With a View to the Improvement of Country Residences* (New York: Orange Judd Agricultural Book Publisher, 1865), 329.

3. A. J. Davis, *Rural Residences* (New York: Alexander Jackson Davis, 1837), vol. VII leaf 31.

4. Richard Olsen, *Log Houses of the World* (New York: Abrams, 2006), 16-19.

Ames Gate Lodge

1. William H. Pierson, Jr., "The Beauty of a Belief: The Ames Family, Richardson, and Unitarianism," in *H.H. Richardson : The Architect, His Peers, and Their Era*, ed. Maureen Meister (Cambridge: MIT Press, 1999), xxvi-xxvii.

2. Margaret Henderson Floyd, *Henry Hobson Richardson: A Genius for Architecture* (New York: Monacelli Press, 1997), 183.

3. Floyd 191-192.

General Charles G. Loring House

1. Benjamin Ives Gilman, "Charles Greely Loring," in *Museum of Fine Arts, Boston: Twenty-Seventh Annual Report for the Year 1902* (Cambridge: The University Press, 1903), 4.

2. Gilman 10.

3. Robert Haven Schauffler, "Unique Mount Desert," *The Century Magazine*, August 1911: 478.

Camp Pine Knot

1. Seneca Ray Stoddard, *The Adirondacks* (Glen Falls, NY: Seneca Ray Stoddard, 1881), 122.

2. "Charms of the Adirondacks," *The New York Times*, 22 July 1894, 9.

3. A. J. Downing, *The Architecture of Country Houses* (New York: D. Appleton & Co., 1859), 123.

4. A. J. Downing, *A Treatise on the Theory and Practice of Landscape Gardening, Adapted to North America; With a View to the Improvement of Country Residences* (New York: Orange Judd Agricultural Book Publisher, 1865), 393.

The Kildare Club

1. Paul Schneider, *The Adirondacks: a History of America's First Wilderness* (New York: Henry Holt & Company, 1997), 244.

2. Cleveland Amory, *The Last Resorts* (New York: Harper & Brothers, 1948), 370.

3. Harvey H. Kaiser, *Great Camps of the Adirondacks* (Boston: David R. Godine, 1982), 135-6.

4. Kaiser 146.

5. Daniel J. Friedman, "The Kildare Club," *ALA News* (2006): 6.

6. Friedman 8.

Camp Topridge

1. Mildred Phelps Stokes Hooker, *Camp Chronicles* (Blue Mountain Lake, NY: Adirondack Museum, 1964), 26.

2. Lee Manchester, "Two Camps on Osgood Pond, Part I," *Lake Placid News*, 21 July 2006: www.adirondackconnections.com/Yoga/060 721%20VLP%20Osgood%20tour%20(1).pdf

3. White Pine Camp (1907) and Northbrook Lodge (1920) as described in: Lee Manchester, "Two Camps on Osgood Pond, Part II," *Lake Placid News*, 28 July 2006: www.adirondackconnections. com/Yoga/060721%20VLP%20Osgood%20tour%20(2).pdf

4. "Mrs. Post's Magnificent World," *Life* vol. 59 no. 19 (5 November 1965): 68.

5. Patricia Leigh Brown, "Out-Twigging the Neighbors; In the Adirondacks, Great Camps Are Sprouting Again," *The New York Times*, 23 October 1997, F1.

6. "Mrs. Marjorie Merriweather Post Is Dead at 86," *The New York Times*, 13 September 1973, 50.

7. Nancy Rubin, *American Empress: The Life and Times of Marjorie Merriweather Post* (New York: Villard Books, 1995), 225.

8. "Mrs. Post's Magnificent World," 66.

9. Harold Faber, "State Sells Its Lavish Camp in Adirondacks for $911,000," *The New York Times*, 1 August 1985, B2.

10. James Howard Kunstler, "For Sale," *The New York Times*, 18 June 1989, section 6, 22.

11. Brown F1.

Wawapek Farm

1. James A. Hijiya, "Four Ways of Looking at a Philanthropist," *Proceedings of the American Philosophical Society* vol. 124 no. 6 (17 December 1980): 405.

2. Priscilla de Forest Williams, *The Story of Wawapek, 1898-1998* (Cold Spring Harbor: private printing, 1998), 2.

3. Craig Gilborn, *Adirondack Camps: Homes Away from Home, 1850-1950* (Syracuse: Adirondack Museum/Syracuse University Press, 2000), 192.

4. Williams 5.

Old Faithful Inn

1. Ruth Quinn, *Weaver of Dreams: The Life and Architecture of Robert C. Reamer* (Gardiner, MT: Leslie & Ruth Quinn, Publishers, 2004), 40.

2. Chris Magoc, *Yellowstone: the Creation and Selling of an American Landscape, 1870-1903* (Albuquerque: University of New Mexico Press, 1999), 110.

3. Quinn 7.

4. "The Railways and the California Exhibition," *Railway Age Gazette* vol. 59 no. 12 (17 September 1915): 500.

5. Christine Macy and Sarah Bonnemaison, *Architecture and Nature: Creating the American Landscape* (New York: Routledge, 2003), 84.

Charles Millard Pratt House

1. The term "ultimate bungalow" was popularized by its use as a chapter title in Randell L. Makinson's *Greene & Greene: Architecture as a Fine Art* (Salt Lake City: Peregrine Smith, 1977).

2. Norval White and Elliot Willensky, *AIA Guide to New York City* (New York: Crown Publishers, 2000), 740.

3. Wesley Haynes, "The Adirondack Camp in American Architecture," *Adirondack Camps Theme Study*: (www.nps.gov/nhl/themes/Architecture/2camp.pdf, 2000): 12.

4. Craig Gilborn, *Adirondack Camps: Homes Away from Home, 1850-1950* (Syracuse: Adirondack Museum/Syracuse University Press, 2000), 252-53.

5. Robert B. MacKay, Anthony K. Baker, and Carol A. Traynor, eds., *Long Island Country Houses and Their Architects, 1860-1940* (New York: Society for the Preservation of Long Island Antiquities/W. W. Norton, 1997), 243.

6. Edward R. Bosley provides the most detailed account to date of the early lives of the Greene brothers in *Greene & Greene* (London: Phaidon Press, 2000), 8-21.

7. Pamela W. Fox, *North Shore Boston: Country Houses Of Essex County, 1865-1930* (New York: Acanthus Press, 2005), 69.

8. L. Morgan Yost, "Greene & Greene of Pasadena," *The Journal of the Society of Architectural Historians* vol. 9 no. 1/2 (March-May 1950): 13.

THE POINT (FORMERLY CAMP WONUNDRA)

1. Harvey H. Kaiser, *Great Camps of the Adirondacks* (Boston: David R. Godine, 1982), 69.

2. Kaiser 164.

FALLINGWATER

1. Cynthia Zaitzevsky, *The Architecture of William Ralph Emerson: 1833-1917* (Cambridge: Fogg Museum, Harvard University, 1969), 25-26.

2. Vincent J. Scully Jr., *The Shingle Style and The Stick Style: Architectural Theory and Design from Downing to the Origins of Wright* (New Haven: Yale University Press, 1955), 159-161.

3. Franz Schulze, *Philip Johnson: Life and Work* (Chicago: University of Chicago Press, 1994), 222.

4. Franklin Toker, *Fallingwater Rising: Frank Lloyd Wright, E. J. Kaufman and America's Most Extraordinary House* (New York: Alfred A. Knopf, 2003), 141.

5. Mark Girouard, "The House and the Natural Landscape: A Prelude to Fallingwater," in *Fallingwater, a Frank Lloyd Wright Country House*, Edgar Kaufmann (New York: Abbeville Press, 1986), 23.

FORTUNE ROCK

1. Joseph B. Thomas, "A Personal Remembrance of Fortune Rock," *GA Houses*, 1982, 11: 15.

2. George Howe, "Some Experiences and Observations of an Elderly Architect," *Perspecta 2, The Yale Architectural Journal* (New Haven, 1953), 4.

3. Thomas 19-20.

WHARTON ESHERICK'S STUDIO

1. Wendy Noonan, "Antiques: A Pioneer And a Rebel, Still a Secret," *The New York Times*, 23 May 2003, E37.

2. Walter Rendell Story, "Decorative Art: Exhibit at Fair," *The New York Times*, 19 May 1940, 51.

3. Story, 51.

4. Arthur J. Pulos, *The American Design Adventure: 1940-1975* (Cambridge: M.I.T. Press, 1988), 7.

MANITOGA

1. Russel Wright, *Russel Wright: Good Design is for Everyone* (New York: Universe, 2001), 67.

2. Donald Albrecht, Robert Schonfeld, and Lindsay Stamm Shapiro, *Russel Wright: Creating American Lifestyle* (New York: Smithsonian Institution/ Abrams, 2001), 116.

3. A. J. Downing, *A Treatise on the Theory and Practice of Landscape Gardening, Adapted to North America; With a View to the Improvement of Country Residences* (New York: Orange Judd Agricultural Book Publisher, 1865), 32.

ROLAND TERRY'S HOUSE

1. Justin Henderson, *Roland Terry: Master Northwest Architect* (Seattle: University of Washington Press, 2000), 37.

2. Jeffrey Karl Ochsner, ed., *Shaping Seattle Architecture: A Historical Guide to the Architects* (Seattle: University of Washington Press, 1994), 228.

3. Henderson 17.

4. "Unloading the Ark," *Time* vol. 85 (5 February 1965): http://www.time.com/time/magazine/art cle/0,9171,839254,00.html

5. Henderson 112-113.

6. Richard Olsen, *Log Houses of the World* (New York: Abrams, 2006), 134.

7. Jeffrey Karl Ochsner suggested to the author that the roof of Roland Terry's house was inspired by an earlier sod-roofed house on Lopez Island, one that Lionel Pries designed for Richard and Ruth Lea in the early 1950s.

8. Marc-Antoine Laugier, *An Essay on Architecture* trans. Wolfgang and Anni Herrmann (Los Angeles: Hennessy and Ingalls, 1977), 11.

SPRUCE LODGE

1. Joseph Giovannini, "Miracle on 34th Street: Robert A. M. Stern Dramatically Reinvents a Rooftop Shed for Himself in Manhattan," *Architectural Digest* vol. 64 no. 7 (July 2007): 32-41.

2. Franz Schulze, *Philip Johnson: Life and Work* (Chicago: University of Chicago Press, 1996), 333.

3. Mark Alden Branch, "Blast from the Past," *Yale Alumni Magazine* vol. 62 (March 1999): 24.

4. Luis F. Rueda, ed., *Robert A. M. Stern: Buildings and Projects 1981-1985* (New York: Rizzoli, 1986), 6-7.

RUSTIC REDUX

1. Stephen Drucker, "Arts and Crafts Cabin: An Architect's One-Room Retreat in New York," *Architectural Digest* vol. 53 no. 6 (June 1996): 158-161, 202.

A MODERN LOG CABIN

1. Paul Goldberger, "Skyscrapers Battle It Out Near Carnegie Hall," *The New York Times*, 21 October 1990, section 2, 38.

2. Millard F. Hearn, *Ideas That Shape Buildings* (Cambridge: MIT Press, 2003), 180.

LEDGE HOUSE

1. Edmund F. Wehrle, *Catoctin Mountain Park: A Historic Resource Survey*, March 2000: http://www.nps.gov/archive/cato/hrs/hrs5a.htm

2. U.S. Department of the Interior, National Park Service, *A Study of the Park and Recreation Problem of the United States* (Washington, D.C.: Government Printing Office, 1941): 4.

3. Oscar Riera Ojeda, ed., *Ledge House: Bohlin Cywinski Jackson* (Gloucester, MA: Rockport Publishers, 1999), 20.

4. Riera Ojeda 20.

LONG RESIDENCE

1. Theresa Morrow," Blending In—Jim Cutler's Designs Admit Up Front That We Are Visitors On This Planet," *The Seattle Times*, 8 July 1990: http://community.seattletimes.nwsource.com/archive/?date=19900708&slug=1081070

2. Morrow.

3. Victoria Medgyesi, "Long Residence," *Architectural Record* vol. 194 no. 01 (January 2006): 163.

RIDGE HOUSE

1. Dung Ngo, ed., *Tom Kundig: Houses* (New York: Princeton Architectural Press, 2006), 48.

2. Henry Matthews, *Kirtland Cutter: architect in the land of promise* (Seattle: University of Washington Press, 1998), 155-156, 300-303.

3. Tony Evans, "A Moving Experience: Tom Kundig designs Sun Valley Center for the Arts' new facility," *Idaho Arts Quarterly* vol. 1 no.26 (2 September-1 December 2008): 18.

INDEX

For my parents, John and Leta

ACKNOWLEDGMENTS

THE OWNERS of many of the properties pictured in these pages welcomed me into their private retreats, in exchange for a pledge of respect for their anonymity. I received enthusiastic cooperation from the following administrators and caretakers at these locations: Jack Mowatt at Langwater; Lynne Warren of the Friends of the Gen. Charles G. Loring House; Jack C. Sheltmire at Camp Huntington, aka Camp Pine Knot; Jay Eseltine at the Kildare Club; Sue Jackman at Camp Topridge; David Dwyer at Wawapek Farm; Bill Moses at the Charles Millard Pratt House; Ardythe Wendt, Karen Low, and Tom Mesereau at the Old Faithful Inn; Phillip Wood of the Garrett Hotel Group, Simone Rathlé of simoneink, and John Graham, the manager of The Point; Clinton Piper at Fallingwater; Gary Ruff, ASID, at Fortune Rock; Kitty McCullough, Executive Director, and Margaret Doyle, Co-President of the Board of Directors, of Manitoga; Joe Goldberg at the Roland Terry House; Nancy Schultz at Spruce Lodge; Netty Azevedo at Rustic Redux; Michelle Corley and Eric Ohmart in Jackson, Wyoming; Greg Currey, the builder of Ledge House; LuAnn Foster at the Long Residence; and Sheri Rasmussen at Ridge House.

The principals and staff of the following architectural firms helped in arranging access to homes they had designed, and answered my many questions about their designs: Robert A. M. Stern, Roger Seifter, and Peter Morris Dixon of Robert A. M. Stern Architects; Alan Shope of Shope Reno Wharton; Robert Charney, formerly of Cesar Pelli and Associates; Peter Bohlin of Bohlin Cywinski Jackson; and Tom Kundig of Olson Sundberg Kundig Allen.

Much of my research occurred at the Avery Architectural Library at Columbia University, where Janet Parks was unstintingly helpful. Angela Donnelley of the Adirondack Museum and Sylvia Inwood of the Detroit Institute of Arts provided period illustrations for the Introduction. Ruth and Mansfield Bascom, daughter and son-in-law of Wharton Esherick, shared their memories of the sculptor. At Topridge, the anecdotes of Lawrence Lester brought to life the camp's heyday under Marjorie Merriweather Post.

A photographer could wish for no finer assistant and travel companion than Mark Silva. Jeff Gandy created revelatory scans of the film I sent to West Coat Imaging. Charlotte Staub brought elegant good sense and stoic patience to her book design. At Rizzoli, publisher Charles Miers was quick to recognize the promise of a project tracing the evolution of rustic architecture. David Morton, associate publisher for architecture, distinguished the forest from the trees with laconic clarity, while editor Douglas Curran cleared thickets of underbrush in readying the book for production.